Mark Carwardine is a zoologist, writer, broadcaster and photographer. He worked in WWF-UK's Conservation Department for six years. Since then he has worked for the Nairobi-based United Nations Environment Programme, as resident Science Writer, and as a consultant to The World Conservation Union (IUCN), in Switzerland. He went freelance in 1986. A frequent contributor to radio and television programmes, he has written more than 20 books on a variety of travel, wildlife and conservation subjects, and numerous articles for newspapers and magazines.

THE WWF ENVIRONMENT HANDBOOK

MARK CARWARDINE

ILLUSTRATED BY
DIANA LEADBETTER

An OPTIMA book

© World Wide Fund for Nature, 1990

First published in 1990 by
Macdonald Optima, a division of
Macdonald & Co. (Publishers) Ltd

A member of Maxwell Macmillan Pergamon Publishing Corporation

British Library Cataloguing in Publication Data
Carwardine, Mark
  WWF environment handbook.
  1. Environment. Conservation
  I. Title   II. World Wide Fund for Nature
  333.7²

  ISBN 0-356-18839-6

Macdonald & Co. (Publishers) Ltd
Orbit House
1 New Fetter Lane
London
EC4A 1AR

Typeset in Ehrhard by
Leaper & Gard Ltd, Bristol, England

Printed on recycled paper and bound in Great Britain by
The Guernsey Press Co. Ltd., Guernsey, Channel Islands.

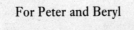

For Peter and Beryl

CONTENTS

ACKNOWLEDGEMENTS

I have been fortunate in having the help and encouragement of a number of people during the research and writing of this book. I would especially like to thank Harriet Griffey, for her infinite patience and enthusiasm. David Symes took great care in editing the final draft. Ian McIntyre kindly approached me to write the book in the first place and was supportive throughout. Pat Harrison helped in umpteen ways, always willingly and with incredible efficiency. Nick Middleton assisted with the research, commented on several draft chapters and discussed ideas at great length. Tessa Robertson, Cassandra Phillips, Mark Halle, Peter Ramshaw, Chris Tydeman and James Martin-Jones all kindly gave their time to comment on various subjects. Doreen Montgomery provided invaluable support. And Debra Taylor slipped food trays under the study door and tolerated my long working hours yet again.

☙ INTRODUCTION

WWF

If we can stop the sky turning into a microwave oven, we will still face the prospect of living in a garbage dump.

HRH Prince Charles

This is a book about human survival. As our population grows, and as we drive animals and plants to extinction, drain wetlands, throw toxic wastes into the sea, pollute the atmosphere, poison drinking water and exhaust the soils, we are destroying the planet's life-support system and threatening the future of all life on Earth.

It is also a book about caring for the environment. We are creating an artificial world motivated by material wealth and economics and, in the process, we are losing touch with nature. 'What is there to life if a man cannot hear the lonely cry of the whip-poor-will, or the arguments of the frogs around a pond at night?' wrote Chief Seattle in 1854.

Only a few years ago, the environmental movement was considered to be rather cranky. It was placed in the same category of eccentrics as the people who have been wandering around for decades with sandwich boards proclaiming 'The End of the World is Nigh'.

It sounds melodramatic but, ironically, the conservation warning is very similar. The fundamental difference is that it should be taken seriously: the future of life on Earth really is under threat.

The facts and figures of what we are doing to the environment are so formidable that they strain our ability to believe: 40 hectares of tropical rainforest destroyed *every minute*; 1,000 different animals and plants becoming extinct every year; a massive hole in the ozone layer, the size of the United States; and so the catalogue of destruction continues.

Yet we lull ourselves into a false sense of security by believing that, somehow, nature will cope with the damage and cover up our mistakes. But the fact that we have 'got away with it' so far should not make us complacent. Nature's resilience is remarkable – but there is a limit to how far it can be stretched. There are indications that we may be very close to that limit already.

Despite the urgent need for action, decision-makers all too often adopt a 'wait-and-see' approach, calling for more research as a decoy to avoid doing something positive. Do we know for sure that rain-forests are disappearing so rapidly? Are minke whales really threatened with extinction? What other forms of atmospheric pollution are causing 'acid rain damage'? These gaps in our knowledge make convenient political excuses. But time is not on our side.

Fortunately, attitudes are changing. There are even politicians with genuine concerns about what is happening – and, of course, many others who realise that there are votes in saving the Earth.

A chain of events – literally within the last two or three years – has increased the number of 'green votes' dramatically. In particular, there was the discovery of the hole in the ozone layer, the unprecedented scientific consensus on global warming, the seal virus in the North Sea and the elephant population crash in Africa. These events have prac-tically forced people to pay attention.

But there are signs that conservation is becoming the fad of the nineties. This could be dangerous, because a fad, by definition, is something that many people are interested in *for a short time*. If we are to tackle the world's environmental problems successfully, we must change our whole way of thinking in order to make conservation a natural part of daily life – not just during the nineties, but forever.

The aim of *The WWF Environment Handbook* is to show where we have gone wrong in the past and how we must change for the future. It is a book for people of all ages, and all nationalities, since managing the Earth wisely requires the determination and perseverance of everyone.

1 ANTARCTICA

Antarctica is the coldest and windiest place in the world. It is too inhospitable for permanent human settlement and so remote that few people will ever be able to go there. So why is it a source of endless concern and controversy?

There are many reasons but, in short, Antarctica is unique. Politically, it belongs to every country in the world rather than to any one in particular. Biologically, it is the largest wildlife sanctuary on earth – a rich feeding ground for whales and millions of seals, penguins and other animals. It is also a critical component in the world's weather system and an invaluable open-air laboratory for monitoring global pollution. But perhaps most significant of all, it is the last virtually unspoilt continent in the world.

So far, Antarctica has escaped most of the destructive human activities that afflict almost everywhere else. But there is growing concern for its future. As scarce resources elsewhere in the world become even scarcer, governments and businesses are looking to Antarctica for new supplies of food and mineral wealth. Given the chance, to meet their short-term economic needs, some would plunder these resources regardless. Others would prefer a longer-term approach, managing the resources wisely.

But many experts believe that, if we do not care for Antarctica in its entirety, we may not preserve it at all. The future of the continent has become almost a choice between material and spiritual values – and one of the great issues of the world today.

WHAT IS ANTARCTICA?

The Antarctic shares several features in common with its counter-part, the Arctic. They are both cold, with a large permanent ice-cover and continuous periods of darkness in winter and daylight in summer.

But there the similarities end. The Arctic is essentially an ocean surrounded by land. It has extensive ice-free areas, and is home to a great diversity of wildlife, large communities of Inuit and Yupik peoples, and many modern settlements. In contrast, the Antarctic is an island, separated from all other continents by a wide sea. It has very few ice-free areas, is one of the most inhospitable places for wildlife on earth, and is so remote and environmentally hostile that no human had set eyes on it until 1820.

A continent of superlatives
The sheer beauty of Antarctica is mind-boggling. The continent itself is roughly circular with a spindly arm, called the Antarctic Peninsula, reaching northwards towards Tierra del Fuego. South America is the nearest landmass, nearly 1,000 kilometres away. Covering some 10 per cent of the earth's land surface, the continent itself has a diameter of about 4,500 kilometres and an area of 14 million square kilometres. This makes it considerably larger than either the United States or Europe, and twice the size of Australia.

Its average height is three times that of any other continent and its highest peak, the Vinson Massif, soars to 5,139 metres. Winds gust at up to 320 kph and temperatures have been known to plummet to as low as minus 89.6°C.

All but 2 per cent of the continent is permanently concealed under a huge icecap which averages over a kilometre-and-a-half in thick-ness. The ice is so heavy that it has depressed about one-third of Antarctica to below sea-level. If it were to melt it would reveal a much smaller landmass of some 7 million square kilometres and the meltwater would raise the level of the world's oceans by between 50 and 60 metres.

Ninety per cent of the planet's freshwater is locked in this icecap. But Antarctica receives little more precipitation than many deserts, with an average of less than 15 centimetres of rain or snow every year.

Surrounding the continent is a frozen sea that varies in area from 2.6 million square kilometres in summer to 18 million square kilometres in winter. Beyond the ice are the stormy waters of the vast Southern Ocean, which encircles Antarctica in a continuous ring several hundred kilometres wide. Connecting with the Pacific, Indian and Atlantic Oceans to the north, it isolates the continent from their warmer waters. This meeting point, called the Antarctic Convergence, is the ecologically defined northern boundary of the Antarctic.

Early theories about Antarctica

There was speculation about the presence of Antarctica for more than a thousand years before it was discovered. It really became a subject of hot debate when Pythagoras postulated, as early as the sixth century BC, that the earth was round. Until then, it was assumed to be flat, in which case there could be no southern hemisphere and therefore no southern landmass.

Greek philosophers were keen to satisfy a sense of symmetry and decided that, if the earth was indeed round, there must be a southern continent to balance the weight of lands known to exist in the north. But rumours of intense heat and fearsome monsters on this unknown continent discouraged any attempts to search for it.

Aristotle later reasoned that, since the northern hemisphere lay under Arktos, the brightest constellation in the northern night skies, the unknown land in the south must be its total opposite – Antarktikos. New theories about the nature of Antarktikos evolved in the 15th century, by which time European explorers had not fallen off the edge of the earth and most people had accepted that it was round. This stimulated intense interest in what the southern continent might be like.

People and exploration

Expedition after expedition was sent in search of Antarctica but, as recently as 1819, no one had found it. The Russian explorer Thaddeus von Bellingshausen eventually sighted the continent on 27 January 1820 although, at the time, he did not know what he was looking at. It was a remarkable coincidence because, three days later, and unbeknown to him, an expedition led by British Captain Edward Bransfield also made a sighting 1,995 kilometres away.

The first landing was probably not until January 1895, when a Norwegian whaling party stepped ashore beneath Cape Adare in Victoria Land. But no one ventured beyond the shoreline. By the turn of the century, however, the world was witnessing the extra-ordinary acts of bravery and endurance by legendary Antarctic explorers such as Scott, Shackleton and Amundsen. They thrust Antarctica into modern consciousness with a vengeance and, within 50 years, the continent was well explored and mapped. Scientists were being sent to the region in droves. The largest expedition was the US Navy's post-war Operation Highjump (1946–7). Planned primarily as a testing and training exercise, it was composed of 13 ships, 23 aircraft and more than 4,700 personnel.

There have been bases in Antarctica since 1899, when two temporary prefabricated wooden huts were erected by a Norwegian explorer. More permanent bases were established in the 1940s, to provide some form of regular presence and activity – not for gradual human settlement but to add weight to any future disputes over sovereignty claims.

There are currently more than 60 year-round scientific bases on Antarctica and the surrounding islands. These are populated by 800 people in the winter and as many as 3,000 during the brief southern summer. The largest is the huge American McMurdo Base, on Ross Island. It is primarily a scientific establishment, but is home to as many navy personnel as scientists. Like a small town, with a popul-ation of up to 800 in the summer, it has a bank, a small hotel and its own airport built on the ice. There is even a base at the South Pole.

Some bases encourage families to live there, and the first baby to be born in the Antarctic, in January 1978, was an Argentinian.

WHY IS ANTARCTICA SO IMPORTANT?

Antarctica has attracted international attention for centuries, primarily from people interested in making money out of its rich resources. But public opinion about some of the proposals for its future has swung from indifference to outrage with the growing real-isation that it is of more long-term value to the world if left untouched.

The largest wildlife sanctuary on earth
Fifty million years ago Antarctica had a temperate climate. It was

covered in a luxuriant vegetation and inhabited by many large animals. But as the weather deteriorated, its wildlife gradually disappeared. Life still retains a tenuous foothold there, despite the persistent cold, the isolation and the short summer season, but it is a precarious existence.

There are no polar bears or musk ox. With few exceptions, the land animals are confined to microbes and small invertebrates; there are more than 240 different parasites, protozoans, rotifers, nematodes, tardigrades, springtails, crustaceans, midges and mites. Most of these live in the moss beds and meltwater ponds and lakes of the Antarctic Peninsula and nearby islands. The largest permanent inhabitant is a wingless fly, less than half an inch long. Few of the others are visible with the naked eye – you need a magnifying glass or a microscope to see them properly.

Apart from snow algae, plant life is limited to the ice-free areas, yet even most of these are rather bare and lack visible vegetation. There are only two native vascular plants – a grass and a pearlwort – though neither survives on the continent itself. There are also some 200 lichens (including one which grows on rocks only 420 kilometres from the South Pole), 85 mosses, 28 toadstools, 25 liverworts, plus unknown numbers of algae and microorganisms such as bacteria, fungi and yeasts.

None of these make Antarctica the greatest wildlife sanctuary on earth, nor are they likely to arouse much sympathy from politicians or oil barons. But the surrounding seas cover more than twice the area of the land and this meagre assortment of terrestrial life is in striking contrast to the abundant wildlife of the Southern Ocean.

At first glance, the most important animals in the Antarctic seas look rather boring and insignificant. No more than 7.5 centimetres long, they are shrimp-like creatures called krill. They feed on microscopic floating plants, or phytoplankton, which thrive in these nutrient-rich waters. For some strange reason, krill are heavier than water and, to remain afloat, themselves, have to paddle constantly.

But for all their faults krill are full of protein and, directly or indirectly, support all the whales, seals and penguins of the Antarctic. They are so numerous, sometimes forming dense swarms more than a kilometre-and-a-half across and 18 metres deep, that their total weight probably exceeds that of any other animal in the world. One record-breaking super-swarm, found near Elephant Island, was estimated to contain an incredible 2.54 million tonnes of the animals.

The swarming habits of krill make them easy prey for other Antarctic wildlife. Humpback, fin, blue, sei, minke and southern right whales capture them simply by swimming through the swarms with their mouths wide open. They sometimes also lunge forward, skim along the surface, or rush on the hapless animals from below. With every gulp of krill, they take in an enormous mouthful of water which has to be sieved through special plates before the animals are ready to swallow. A 24-metre blue whale swallows around 4 tonnes of krill – more than four million of them – every day.

Many other animals take advantage of these rich pickings. Krill makes up nearly 80 per cent of the diet of some 100 million Antarctic birds. Forty-three different species breed within the limits of the Antarctic Convergence, most of them seabirds. Fewer than a quarter of these breed on the Antarctic continent itself, although one, the emperor penguin, is the only large animal which remains there throughout the long months of winter darkness.

Antarctic seals probably eat more than 150 million tonnes of krill every year, the Antarctic fur seal and, despite its name, the crabeater seal feeding almost exclusively on krill. Crabeaters are possibly the commonest large mammals on earth; some estimates put their total population in the Antarctic as high as 30 million, although a more recent study put it at nearer 4.7 million. Leopard seals also include krill as a major part of their diet, although they are opportunistic predators and take a wide variety of prey, including other seals.

There are a few mammals or birds in the Antarctic which do not eat krill, but even these belong to food webs which are built around the ubiquitous animals. Krill fall prey to many kinds of squid and fish which, in turn, are eaten by Ross, Weddell and southern elephant seals, sperm whales, four-tooth and bottlenose whales, and various dolphins. Even killer whales, which are common animals in the region, hunting mainly seals and penguins, would be absent without krill.

This is, of course, a simplification of what happens in the Southern Ocean food web. But it does illustrate the fact that most of the larger animals are totally, partially or indirectly dependent on krill for food. It forms the basis of a rich wildlife paradise on the grandest scale. Without krill, the Antarctic ecosystem would collapse.

Regulating the world's climate

One of the driving forces of the world's weather system is the great temperature difference between the tropics and the poles.

The tilt of the earth on its axis is such that more of the sun's energy is received in some parts of the world than in others. This solar energy is plentiful in the tropics, where it is absorbed quickly by the seas and landmasses, causing them to heat up. But Antarctica's permanent covering of snow and ice reflect 80 per cent of its meagre solar energy back into space. For most of the year, Antarctica actually loses more heat than it gains from the sun.

But heat is constantly being redistributed around the world by the motion of the atmosphere and the oceans. This prevents the Antarctic from getting colder and colder and, at the same time, counterbalances the heat gains of the tropics. These huge transfers of energy, from one part of the world to another, establish an equilibrium which stops the earth either warming up or cooling down.

The cold Antarctic plays such a crucial role in this system that any significant change in its icecap is likely to have disastrous results.

Monitoring global change

There is no doubt that we are poisoning our planet. But what are the consequences? The best way of finding out is to monitor pollution levels, somewhere in the world, under pristine conditions that can be used as a standard for comparison.

The Antarctic is ideal. Its ice sheet is the cleanest natural area left on earth and its remoteness from human populations and industry means that it is far removed from the main sources of the planet's environmental problems. None the less, it still picks up the effects of human activity elsewhere in the world, proving that today's pollution problems really are making a global impact.

It was research in the Antarctic which first warned of the harm man-made chlorofluorocarbons (CFCs) were doing to the ozone layer. Antarctic research has also shown that, in the last 200 years, there has been a 25 per cent increase in carbon dioxide levels in the atmosphere.

Early warning systems such as these are essential for monitoring the human-made global changes of the modern world. Such information may give us the time necessary to take evasive action.

WHAT ARE THE MAIN THREATS?

Antarctica's wildlife has been exploited for many years, with far-reaching consequences. But, as if we need an indelible reminder of continued human greed, there are plans to take even larger catches and to begin commercial exploration of the continent's suspected mineral resources. These plans are based on little or no information. But they appear to be making convincing political arguments and could result in penguin colonies being replaced with industrial settlements, or pristine ice and snow with oil slicks.

Oil and mineral exploitation

Antarctica is believed to contain large quantities of oil. A Soviet geologist has predicted that its oil resources exceed those of Alaska, while Gulf Oil estimated, in 1979, that the accessible continental shelves could contain 50,000 million barrels of oil – and probably much more. Compared with proven reserves elsewhere, this is a considerable amount.

There is no conclusive evidence for these estimates, but enough to convince oil companies and governments that the enormous cost of exploring Antarctica's oil reserves would be worthwhile. The oil industry has now considerable experience of drilling in the Arctic, and the technology for deep-sea drilling is advancing rapidly, so much of the expertise in overcoming similar obstacles is already there.

In theory, commercial mineral exploration in Antarctica has been voluntarily prohibited for many years. But there is a fine line between this and geophysical scientific research, with the result that the mineral potential of the continent and its offshore islands has actually been explored for some time. The first stage in serious exploration began in 1981, with a sophisticated seismic survey by the Japan National Oil Corporation to evaluate the oil potential of the Bellingshausen Sea. Other governments have done seismic work in recent years and there is mounting pressure for commercial seismic projects to be allowed.

Drilling for oil is probably the greatest threat currently facing Antarctica. It would involve an influx of large numbers of personnel, increased shipping operations, the importation of massive amounts of equipment and the construction of substantial structures and facilities along the coast. There is very little ice-free land in Antarctica not already occupied by breeding birds or scientific stations. It is not hard to guess who would be most likely to win a competition for the most attractive locations.

Inevitably, there would be oil spills. The *Exxon Valdez* disaster illustrated all too clearly the consequences of allowing huge oil tankers into remote and vulnerable places. On 24 March 1989 the tanker ran on to a submerged reef in Prince William Sound, Alaska. Over the following weeks, 50 million litres of oil leaked from the ship and spread over thousands of square kilometres of previously pristine beaches, shoreline and islands.

Enormous tankers would be required to make the journey to Antarctica worthwhile. Yet there have been several accidents there already – with small ships involved only in benign research projects and tourism – which ought to be grim reminders of the shipping hazards in Antarctic waters. For example, on 28 January 1989 an Argentinian ship, the *Bahia Paraiso*, ran aground on well-charted rocks off the Antarctic Peninsula. It was carrying supplies and tourists to Argentinian bases. The passengers and crew were rescued but the ship sank and nearly half of its 1,136,500 litres of diesel fuel and 150 barrels of jet oil spilled into the sea. The logistics of a clean-up were hopeless, with the remoteness of the area and the lack of facilities nearby. It was a week before oil-spill equipment arrived to start the operation. By this time, the fuel and oil had done untold damage to the local environment and destroyed years of scientific work which relied on a pristine environment. Before the operation could be completed, the brief Antarctic summer drew to a close and the clean-up had to be abandoned.

It is the fact that the Antarctic summer is so short that would make oil drilling particularly dangerous. If a blow-out were not controlled by the end of the season, like the *Bahia Paraiso* it would have to be left unchecked for many months. Oil spills, from rigs or tankers, could become trapped under the ice, or be incorporated into it, making it impossible to return the Antarctic waters to their natural state. A major spill could be a death blow to the struggling whale populations of Antarctica.

Oil is currently attracting the most commercial interest, but there are many other minerals on the continent. These include copper, molybdenum, nickel, chromium, platinum, lead, zinc, silver, tin, gold, coal and iron. Substantial deposits could be hidden beneath thousands of yards of ice but they might still be accessible and, if prices allow, economically viable.

Dust from mining activities – or spilled oil – would have a devastating effect on local wildlife populations. But, more importantly, it would darken the surface of the Antarctic icecap. By lowering its reflectivity and increasing its heat absorption, this could have a significant effect on global weather patterns. If the ice were to melt, the resulting water could affect sea levels and threaten coastal cities in many parts of the world.

After delicate negotiations lasting for almost ten years, an agreement called the Convention on the Regulation of Antarctic Mineral Resource Activities (CRAMRA) has been adopted. This includes strong environmental safeguards but, equally, makes mining and oil development legally possible in Antarctica for the first time.

WWF and other organisations are strongly opposed to CRAMRA, or the Antarctic Minerals Convention as it is more commonly known. A major concern is that it does not provide stringent controls on prospecting. Yet this prospecting is, in itself, dangerous to the Antarctic environment, and also leads the parties down a dangerous path; if a substantial find is made, they will be under enormous pressure from commercial and political interests to allow exploitation. After all, the intention of the agreement is to provide a regime for possible exploitation, not to prevent it in every case.

Several countries have vetoed the Convention. The first was Australia, which called for an Antarctic Wilderness Park in its place. France followed suit, after the Cousteau Foundation organised a petition which received an astonishing 750,000 signatures in only two months. Italy and Belgium have also complained that the Convention does not provide enough protection for the environment, and several other countries, including India and even the Soviet Union, are now likely to join the growing movement against it.

CRAMRA has to be ratified before it comes into force, and it is still being discussed. Fortunately, it is moribund without the ratification of Australia, France and the others. But many nations are undecided about whether or not to endorse it, and several have made no secret of their interest in Antarctica's mineral resources. In particular, there are a number of pro-mining heavyweights, including the United Kingdom, the United States and Japan, which will put tremendous pressure on the others to win their consent. Yet the environmental risks of mining and oil development in Antarctica are so great that such activities should never be allowed.

Hunting and fishing

The early history of wildlife exploitation in the Antarctic is one of wanton slaughter. Seals, whales and penguins were killed in their millions. Today, with one notorious exception – Japanese minke whaling – hunting of this kind has largely been stopped. But there is now concern that growing commercial fishing operations will have grave implications for the entire Antarctic ecosystem.

The first animals to be exploited were the fur seals of South Georgia. Sealing started there in 1790, just 15 years after Captain Cook had discovered the island. By 1822 at least 1.25 million animals had been killed and the Antarctic fur seal was commercially extinct. The sealers then turned their attentions to elephant seals until, by the end of the century, they too had virtually disappeared and the sealing was no longer profitable.

This pattern characteristically followed the discovery of new islands. British and American sealers, seeking valuable furs and oil, indiscriminately wiped out one population after another. Throughout the nineteenth century, repeated sealing expeditions stripped almost every island in the Southern Ocean of its seals.

Hunting for elephant seals resumed in 1910; one million of the animals had been slaughtered, but they were recovering quickly. This time the operations were under the strict supervision of the British administration on South Georgia. The elephant seal population probably could have sustained its new quota system indefinitely. But the sealers worked in conjunction with the South Georgia whaling industry and, when the local whales had been hunted to commercial extinction, both industries abandoned the island in 1964.

No other seals have been hunted on a large scale in Antarctica, although the question of exploitation has arisen several times. Two Soviet vessels killed 4,802 seals of various species in 1986–7, primarily as a commercial harvest, but the logistical problems of such enterprises make them too expensive to be worthwhile.

As a safeguard, there are adequate regulations for seal hunting in the Antarctic. The killing of fur, elephant and Ross seals for commercial purposes is strictly prohibited. There are strict annual quotas for crabeater (175,000), leopard (12,000) and Weddell (5,000) seals, designed to allow a limited take for scientific studies and dog food, and to control commercial harvesting if it is ever resumed.

Whaling operations in the Southern Ocean began properly in 1904, by which time whale populations were already in serious decline in the North Atlantic. Initially, the operations were shore-based and catches had to be towed back for processing. They concentrated on humpback whales, which liked the relatively shallow waters near the stations, but as their numbers declined the whalers were forced to go further and further afield.

Then in 1925 large floating factories were introduced. These were able to haul several whales on board at once for processing at sea, making it possible for the whalers to go anywhere in search of their quarry. Within five years, Britain and Norway had 41 floating factories and more than 200 whale catcher boats in the Antarctic. The most sought-after species was the largest of them all, the blue whale. At the peak of the whaling operations, in the short 1930–1 season, an incredible 30,000 blue whales were killed. In the mid-1930s the Britons and Norwegians were joined by Japanese and German operations and, later, by several other nations. As the blue whale catch declined, the whalers concentrated on other species and, one by one, the Antarctic's great whales were hunted to commercial extinction. Several of them are now undoubtedly in very serious trouble.

There is one smaller whale, the minke, which was not hunted until all its larger relatives had been severely depleted. But after years of exploitation, and in defiance of international regulations, Japan continues to hunt minke whales with its own self-imposed 'scientific research' quotas. For each of the past two years. the whalers have set out for the Antarctic to kill 300 of the animals. But they managed to find 'only' 273 in 1987–8 and 241 in 1988–9.

Penguins were always considered fair game for the whalers and sealers, although they have never been killed in dangerously large numbers. Unable to fly, and always trusting, penguins are easy birds to catch. Their flesh and eggs are tasty, their skins once fetched high prices in the world of fashion and they have layers of fat which provided oil for lighting. During the period 1891–1916 nearly four million king and royal penguins were killed on Macquarie Island for their tiny quantities of oil. This is one of the few example of large-scale penguin harvesting in the Southern Ocean – yet, during the hunting period, the number of penguins in the rookery actually increased. There have been more recent proposals, from the Japanese, to harvest penguins commercially but these have not been carried out.

A far more serious threat – to all Antarctic wildlife – is over-fishing. Fish were first exploited commercially in the Southern Ocean in the mid-1960s, after more than 30 years of repeated trials by a number of nations. An annual peak of 400,000 tonnes, caught mostly by the Soviets, was reached in 1969–70. Nearly all the the catch was a fish called the marbled notothenia, a relative of the Antarctic cod. Since then, icefish have also been taken in large numbers, along with Patagonian hake, blue whiting, lantern fish and others.

Fishing in the Antarctic was effectively unregulated for many years, with the discovery of new stocks characteristically followed by rapid overfishing. Under similar conditions many other, apparently bottomless, stocks of wildlife have disappeared in the past – and Antarctic fish appear to be no exception. They take several years to mature, and have slow growth rates, so are especially vulnerable to fishing, even at apparently 'safe' levels. Since 1969 several populations have declined by as much as 90 per cent, while the Antarctic cod is now commercially extinct. The intensity of fishing has been such that even fish that were caught by mistake – 'vacuumed' up with the target species – are now seriously depleted.

Nowadays there are total bans on fishing for a few of the species in most serious trouble (although these have been vetoed by the Soviet Union) and the annual catch has fallen to around 100,000 tonnes. But all the world's major fishing fleets are working the Antarctic waters and the only way of rebuilding the stocks may be to close the fishery altogether.

Many experts believe that a sizeable krill fishery is destined to take its place. Krill could be one of the planet's largest remaining untapped sources of food and, handled sensibly, might help to feed the overpopulated human world. But the effects of tapping even small quantities are unknown – and experience with the fish should act as a warning.

The first exploratory krill fishing expeditions were made by the Japanese and the Soviets in the early 1960s. The technology for catching, processing and preparing krill for commercial use developed slowly at first, but nowadays krill swarms are detected using high-frequency echo-sounders, and daily catching rates of 100 tonnes per fishing boat are being achieved.

The great difficulty has been in establishing suitable markets for this new food. Initial production of krill paste and cheese was not a commercial success; most of the catch ended up as a food supplement for domestic animals, even though it was too expensive to compete with other types of fishmeal. Much effort has gone into 'peeling' the krill but, again, this is not yet economically viable. More success has been achieved recently in Japan with a variety of krill products, and once these have been developed sufficiently there are plans to increase the krill fisheries dramatically.

Current catch levels are fairly modest, averaging about 400,000 tonnes per year since 1986, and taken mainly from around South Georgia. The main krill fishing nations are still Japan and the Soviet Union, although Chile, South Korea, Poland and others are now involved experimentally. With the collapse of so many traditional fisheries in recent years, because of overfishing and due to their exclusion from territorial waters in temperate latitudes, many other fleets are likely to follow suit.

Concern is not so much for the krill itself but for the impact over-harvesting will inevitably have on other Antarctic wildlife. In particular, it could quickly jeopardise the recovery of endangered whales. The much-reduced whale populations eat at least 100 million tonnes of krill less per year than they did before the whalers took their toll. These 'left-overs' are probably being taken by other krill-eating species, such as seals and penguins, which consequently may be growing in numbers. So competition for krill is already intense in the Southern Ocean, and some scientists believe that even a small annual harvest – under two million tonnes – could swing the balance against the survival of several whale species.

The main difficulty is that there is surprisingly little information on krill. No one knows how many there are, or how they are distributed. We do not even have the facts about their lifespan, breeding rate or growth rate. There could be as many as 650 million tonnes of them in the Antarctic – but, for all we know, an annual harvest of only 0.1 per cent could have disastrous consequences. Much more research is needed to establish safe catch levels, or if, indeed, there should be any krill fishing in the Antarctic at all.

Human settlements

Most of the recognisable damage caused by human activities on Antarctica is around research bases. They compete with wildlife for space and have major problems with waste disposal.

Research bases need level ground, freedom from permanent ice and snow, and good access to the sea in summer. But so do many penguins and seals. When new bases are opened, or old ones expanded, little thought is given to this problem. One base even blasted its way through a penguin colony to make way for an airstrip.

Some of the modern bases are enormous, consisting of many buildings, diesel-powered generators and a year's supply of food. Their rubbish dumps are correspondingly huge. Every year, thousands of tonnes of cargo, and millions of litres of fuel, are brought in. In spite of recent improvements, little of it is ever removed. The ships routinely pump their bilges offshore, and oil slicks are becoming common. A great deal of waste, including human sewage, is dumped straight into the sea, or onto the ice. Underwater photography at the bottom of McMurdo Sound reveals old vehicles, pipes, fuel drums, beer cans and clothing. And at the spectacular Soviet base, perched precariously on top of Mt Lenin, discarded oil drums are casually tossed over the precipice.

There is no easy solution. Even the incineration of combustible materials gives rise to air emissions which could pollute the pristine Antarctic environment. But there is a rule of thumb: everything that is brought into Antarctica must be taken away.

There is a further, albeit potential, problem with human settlements. Wherever people go they have a nasty habit of introducing alien animals and plants that can do massive amounts of damage. Two cats were introduced to Marion Island, in the sub-Antarctic, in

1949. Their descendents, which now are counted in their thousands, kill nearly half a million birds every year and have exterminated the island's diving petrels. Originally, the cats were brought in to control rodents, but they found the birds easier prey.

The Antarctic continent itself has not suffered in this way, although bacteria have been introduced around research bases. But there have been a number of introductions – both intentional and accidental – to islands such as Marion, South Georgia, Macquarie and Kerguelen; cattle, sheep, goats, mouflon, horses, pigs, black and brown rats, mice, rabbits, reindeer and cats have all found their way to these islands over the years. Many of them have become well established. Apart from the obvious damage the animals can do, there are probably many more subtle, and less obvious, effects as well. So it is important that no further introductions are made.

Tourism

It seems extraordinary that people can go on holiday to a land which, for centuries, had been no more than a myth. But tourism in Antarctica is already 25 years old and, with its obvious attractions, may be approaching a rapid phase of expansion. There are even proposals to provide land-based tourist facilities, such as hotels and airstrips, to accommodate the burgeoning tourist operations.

There were occasional tourist flights from South America over the Antarctic Peninsula as early as 1956, but tourism really got underway when the first luxury cruise ships began to visit the Peninsula in 1965. By 1977 jumbo jets were making regular day excursion flights over the continent from Australia and New Zealand.

The problems caused by these trips are a subject of hot debate, although they may be less serious than many people suppose. A typical three-week cruise, for example, may include no more than 20 hours ashore. And it has been said that tourists on Antarctic cruises are often better behaved, and more conservation-minded, than some of the scientific station personnel. But the landing of large groups cannot be supervised properly and may have lasting effects on plants and animals, at least locally. Also, visits to scientific stations are often included in the itineraries and, although these are often welcomed by the scientists, they can cause disruption of work and considerable social stresses.

Perhaps more importantly, dealing with accidents involving tourist ships or aircraft is costly and requires the hazardous and time-consuming use of scarce personnel. In November 1979 an Air New Zealand DC10 crashed into Mount Erebus, killing all 257

people on board. The rescue operation and subsequent investigations disrupted all scientific work at Scott Base and McMurdo
Sound for most of the 1979–80 season, and brought an abrupt end to
these popular tourist flights. So far, thankfully, there have been few
serious accidents in the Antarctic, but in the future they are almost
inevitable if tourist numbers continue to increase.

There is no immediate need to encourage tourism to Antarctica
but, on the other hand, it would be wrong to ban it altogether; as
global citizens, everyone has a right to see it. A solution might be to
develop limited, carefully controlled visits, which could help to
divert the increasing pressure for other, far more damaging, forms of
exploitation.

WHO OWNS ANTARCTICA?

Antarctica belongs to everyone and no one. Many countries believe
that it should be protected as part of the common heritage of
mankind. But others are struggling to control it, or have already
staked a claim to certain sections, perhaps believing that sovereignty
gives an inherent right to its resources.

National claims
There were formal national claims to sections of Antarctica as early
as 1908. Today, seven nations claim sovereignty over different parts
of the continent – Australia, Norway, France, New Zealand, the
United Kingdom, Chile and Argentina. At the Argentinian base of
Esperanza you are even greeted by a sign which says 'Welcome to
Argentina'. Three sectors (Argentina, Chile and the United
Kingdom) overlap each other, yet 15 per cent of the continent, in the
Pacific portion, remains unclaimed.

A number of countries, led by the United States and the Soviet
Union, have expressly declined either to recognise any of these
claims or to make claims of their own. Antarctica is a potential
strategic base from which to mount military operations and, until
1961, there was growing concern that serious military confrontation
might engulf the continent. It would not be absurd to imagine a
conflict more severe than the Falklands War, which itself was
probably as much to do with access to Antarctica as it was with
protecting the rights of the islanders.

Sovereignty is a contentious issue. But everyone currently 'agrees
to disagree', thanks largely to a remarkable international pact called
the Antarctic Treaty.

The Antarctic Treaty

The Antarctic Treaty does not solve the question about who owns Antarctica, but it was established as a device to defuse competition and has frozen all territorial claims. There is now freedom of access to the entire continent.

The Treaty came into force on 23 June 1961. It is open for signature by all nations and now has 39 'members', representing 80 per cent of the human population. Providing a legal framework for all decision-making in the region, it covers the entire area (except for the high seas) south of latitude 60°S.

When the Treaty was agreed, the level and variety of activity in Antarctica was hardly cause for constant vigilance. It was assumed, reasonably enough at the time, that there was nothing of commercial value on the continent. But nowadays there is much more at stake, and Treaty members face new challenges and continually have to adapt to new demands and pressures. To add to these problems, every development within the Treaty system must continue to avoid prejudicing the question of ownership.

Over the years, the Treaty has achieved a great deal, and an impressively high level of cooperation and negotiation has been reached. However, much of its decision-making has been shrouded in secrecy and it does have its shortcomings.

The Treaty states that Antarctica should be used for peaceful purposes only. No military personnel are allowed, except in support of scientific operations. But several governments staff their scientific stations with military personnel, and Argentina goes as far as calling its stations 'military bases'. The Treaty also states that nuclear explosions, and the creation or dumping of radioactive wastes, are prohibited. But the United States was not deterred from building a nuclear power reactor at McMurdo in the 1960s. The reactor was finally shut down in 1972, after years of problems and accidents. Thousands of cubic metres of contaminated earth had to be removed.

The Treaty guarantees the exchange of information and research results. And a body called the Scientific Committee on Antarctic Research (SCAR) was set up, as part of the Treaty system, to help identify and coordinate scientific investigations in Antarctica. But several nations are conducting or planning 'research' of direct relevance to oil and mineral exploitation. It will be interesting to see if they keep the data for themselves.

A wide selection of valuable agreements and guidelines have grown out of the Antarctic Treaty, known collectively as the Antarctic Treaty System. These cover everything from expeditions and research bases to telecommunications and tourism. With their help, substantial progress has been made in protecting the environment. There is, for example, a Convention on the Conservation of Antarctic Marine Living Resources. This has good intentions but has been a failure so far because the Soviet Union vetoes nearly all conservation measures – and these have to be agreed by consensus. There is also a Convention for the Conservation of Antarctic Seals and Agreed Measures for the Conservation of Antarctic Flora and Fauna. There is even a formal system to initiate environmental impact assessments. But this good, basic framework needs to be developed much more to meet the growing pressures facing Antarctica today. There are many loopholes, the agreements are all voluntary (and therefore difficult to enforce) and they are crippled by a lack of basic information.

There have been reports suggesting that the Antarctic Treaty expires after 30 years of operation. This is not true. It could remain in force indefinitely, but a review is possible (and very likely) any time after 1991.

WHAT MUST BE DONE TO PROTECT ANTARCTICA?

There is often a feeling of inevitability about the kind of problems facing Antarctica. In the real world, wild places generally come a distant second to commercial interests and politics. But in this exceptional case the risks of exploitation are simply too great to exchange for a few years' extra supply of raw materials.
- Oil and mineral exploitation must be banned.
- Whales, seals and penguins should be given absolute sanctuary.
- Fish and krill need to be given total protection for a period of years, to give the stocks a chance to recover and to research levels of safe exploitation.
- Tourism must be controlled.
- There should be stricter regulations governing scientific bases.

The World Conservation Union (formerly known as the International Union for Conservation of Nature and Natural Resources, IUCN), WWF's scientific partner, is currently preparing a single, integrated Conservation Strategy for Antarctica, to put to the Antarctic Treaty members. This is essential.

But there can be no half-measures. Many governments and most environmental organisations (including WWF) believe that Antarctica should be established as a World Wilderness Park and given total protection. It is important to the world emotionally and spiritually, as well as for practical reasons.

The idea for a World Park, which would be the first of its kind, was originally mooted in 1972 and then taken formally to an Antarctic Treaty meeting in 1975. It was proposed by New Zealand, which offered to drop its own territorial claims if other nations would follow suit. No one did. But many countries since have expressed a serious interest in the idea.

Is it all pie in the sky? Given past experience, the chances of establishing such a Park may seem remote. But as the late Sir Peter Scott, who worked tirelessly for many years to preserve Antarctica, once said of his hopes for the continent: 'Down the years I have become used to being called an unrealistic idealist, but from time to time events turn out just as one hopes they will.'

WWF believes the best way to save Antarctica – to keep it as the last unspoiled continent – is to make it into a World Park through the international agreement of an environmental protection convention. WWF is mobilising the public to oppose plans by some governments, including Britain, to sign the proposed Antarctic Minerals Convention – which could open the way to exploitation of the continent's mineral resources and the consequent inevitability of environmental pollution.

2
ATMOSPHERIC POLLUTION

WWF

The atmosphere is the thin envelope of gases that surrounds our planet. It is divided into five layers, known as the troposphere, which is nearest to the earth, the stratosphere, mesosphere, thermosphere and, more than 400 kilometres above the surface of the earth, the exosphere.

The actual mixture of gases makes it quite different to the atmosphere of our nearest neighbours in the solar system. Those of Venus and Mars consist predominantly of carbon dioxide, with water vapour, nitrogen, oxygen and other gases accounting for only a few per cent between them. But the earth's atmosphere consists of 78 per cent nitrogen, 21 per cent oxygen and considerably less than 1 per cent carbon dioxide, with very tiny quantities of other gases and variable amounts of water vapour.

The delicate mixture has several functions, apart from providing oxygen for animals to breathe and carbon dioxide for plants to use in photosynthesis. The most important of these are absorbing the lethal ultra-violet rays of the sun and keeping the earth warm.

Environmental scientists have been aware of the fragility of the atmosphere for a long time. But it is only during the last few years that world leaders have begun to acknowledge the serious and widespread atmospheric damage being caused by modern society and industrial processes. These have created three major problems – acid rain, the depletion of the ozone layer and the greenhouse effect. Widely considered to be the most critical environmental issues facing the world today, they are all global in scope and can be solved only by an unprecedented level of international cooperation.

ACID RAIN

Winds are capable of transporting huge quantities of material in the air. They are continually moving gases, plumes of smoke from forest fires, ash from volcanic eruptions and enormous clouds of sand and soil dust from deserts, vast distances around the globe. Dust from the Sahara Desert, for example, is often blown over Europe and even right across the Atlantic as far as the Caribbean and South America.

For centuries people have contributed to the materials being thrown into the atmosphere. But since the industrial revolution (from the mid-18th century onwards) human activities have been emitting so many harmful substances that we are now faced with severe, and sometimes irreversible, atmospheric pollution problems.

The problems really started when coal fires and factory chimneys began to pour an obnoxious mixture of smoke and gases into the air. Unhealthy smogs (which are basically pollution-carrying fogs) became a normal aspect of city life. Then in 1952 London experienced its most notorious pea-souper, as the smogs were commonly called; for nearly a week the city was smothered in a stinking sulphurous cloud that made it impossible to see further than a few metres. It killed 4,000 people and the British government was at last prompted to take action.

New Clean Air Acts were introduced, bringing with them smokeless zones and taller factory chimneys. Many other countries followed suit and city air (for a while at least) was cleared of most visible pollution. Only dirty buildings and monuments remained as grim reminders of how filthy the cities had been. But the problem was not solved by pumping the smoke and gases higher into the atmosphere – they were simply dispersed and diluted. Even with today's chimney-stacks, which are often more than 300 metres high, the pollution does not disappear. It has to go somewhere.

High in the atmosphere it reacts with water and sunlight to form a variety of different acids. These are carried on the wind, often for thousands of miles, before falling to earth in the rain. Sometimes they fall in a variety of other guises, including mist, fog, hail, snow, dew, soot and ash. These invisible poisons are sometimes as acidic as vinegar and staggering quantities fall on many parts of the world, killing wildlife, destroying habitats and damaging buildings.

Dubbed 'acid rain', the harm the pollution is doing has been likened to an ecological holocaust. The exact costs and causes are still being disputed (particularly by certain prevaricating governments) but, meanwhile, the problem is getting worse.

What is the source of acid rain?

The main sources of acid pollution are sulphur dioxide, which oxidises in the atmosphere to form sulphuric acid, and nitrogen oxides, which form nitric acid.

Both of these occur naturally. Sulphur dioxide is produced by volcanoes and microorganisms when they break down organic matter, and through biological processes in the surface layer of the sea. Nitrogen oxides are formed when lightning causes nitrogen and oxygen in the atmosphere to combine, and is also emitted by decaying organic matter. But emissions from a variety of human activities are adding dramatically to the atmospheric levels of these gases. Man-made sources now equal, or outweigh, their natural production.

Electricity generation is the largest single source of acid rain. A large coal-fired power station emits 1 tonne of sulphur dioxide every 5 minutes. But any industrial process which burns fossil fuels (such as coal and oil) contributes to the emissions. A recent unconfirmed report suggests that ships at sea, burning heavy unrefined diesel oils, are also contributing a significant amount.

Worldwide, more than 130 million tonnes of man-made sulphur dioxide is pumped into the atmosphere every year. This probably accounts for half of all the sulphur produced naturally. But the problem is worse in Europe and the industrial regions of eastern North America, where man-made sulphur dioxide probably accounts for as much as 90 per cent of the total production.

Nitrogen oxides, or NO_x as they are commonly known, are produced by all combustion processes. Vehicle exhausts are a major source but the remainder comes from power stations, nitrogenous fertilisers and the burning of forests and tropical grasslands. Worldwide, as much as 36 million tonnes of man-made NO_x is spewed into the atmosphere every year, which effectively doubles the natural emissions.

The effect of acid rain

The levels of acidity in rain and other depositions are measured with the pH scale. This scale ranges from 0, the most acidic, through 7 (which is neutral) to 14, the most alkaline. Lemon juice is acidic, with a pH of 2; milk is slightly acidic, with a pH of 6; and seawater is slightly alkaline, with a pH of 8. Each division on the scale represents a ten-fold increase in acidity or alkalinity; therefore pH 5, for example, is ten times more acidic than pH 6, and 100 times more acidic than pH 7.

Water in the atmosphere is naturally slightly acidic; atmospheric carbon dioxide makes the rain fall as a weak carbonic acid at a pH of between 5 and 6. This natural acidity can be increased by certain events, such as volcanic eruptions and forest fires, which pump large quantities of gases into the atmosphere.

Every ecosystem has a critical load; in other words a certain amount of natural or man-made acid deposition it can take (and neutralise) before being seriously damaged. Some areas, for example where the underlying rock is limestone, can cope with acid rain better than others, because they have a good buffering capacity – the limestone neutralises the acid up to a certain level.

The acid rain itself does not kill animals and plants directly but as a result of a number of different processes. For example, it kills fish by liberating aluminium in the water, which eventually causes a clogging of their gills. In some birds, such as blue tits and great tits, it causes eggshell thinning. And it kills trees by washing nutrients out of the soil and liberating toxic elements, which the trees are tricked into taking up instead of the nutrients.

Millions of hectares of forests, in over 20 countries, have died already as a direct result of acid rain and other air-borne pollutants. Millions more are seriously damaged and will probably die in the near future. Conifers appear to be particularly badly affected: their needles become shorter and less durable; their top buds dry up; the annual growth of shoots becomes shorter; and the tree crown thins out. The main visible symptoms on deciduous trees are discolouration of the leaves, a lack of regeneration and die-back at the crown.

Damage is particularly severe in West Germany, where 50 per cent of the forests are damaged or dying; 40 per cent of the forests in Switzerland are dying and 38 per cent in Sweden. One survey in Britain revealed that 64 per cent of all trees show at least some signs of damage. The effect of acid rain on North America's forests has also been devastating.

Acid rain destroys lakes and rivers as well. Sweden has 90,000 lakes, and 4,000 of them are too acidic (with a pH of less than 5) to support fish or any other aquatic life; a further 18,000 have experienced some acidification and another 20,000 will be affected in the near future. One in five of the lakes in the United States is now fishless for the same reason.

The cultural and financial costs of acid rain damage are also considerable. The Parthenon, in Athens, has suffered more erosion in the past 30 years, due to acid rain, than during the past 2,000 years. In the European Community, the estimated cost of damage to buildings is between US$0.5 and US$2.7 billion annually. And the damage in Poland costs the country roughly 10 per cent of its total national income.

There is, however, one major problem in estimating the financial and environmental costs of acid rain damage: it is extremely difficult to distinguish from damage caused by other natural factors, such as bad weather, pest attack and disease. One reason for this is the way in which acid rain works. It has been likened to the effect of the acquired immune deficiency syndrome (AIDS) on people, which causes a breakdown in the immune system. In the same way, acid rain makes trees more susceptible to natural hazards such as insects, high winds, frost and drought. Other pollutants, such as ground-level ozone, damage trees directly and also make them more vulnerable to some of these hazards; ozone actually accentuates acid rain damage by increasing the loss of nutrients that are leached from the soil.

How can the acid rain problem be solved?

Acid rain is a difficult problem to solve. It is caused by a mixture of human activities, all of which play a major role in modern society; the damage it does is difficult to quantify, or even to identify; and, above all, countries emitting acid rain pollutants often do not suffer the consequences of their own lack of pollution control.

Prevailing winds carry the atmospheric pollution produced in one country across national borders to other countries, often thousands of kilometres away. Two-thirds of the sulphur dioxide emitted from British power stations is exported – often all the way to northern Europe – before it falls to the ground. Similarly, several million tonnes of acid-releasing pollutants are blown across the border from the United States into Canada every year. Bermuda also receives a great deal of acid rain from the United States; the rain there sometimes has a pH of 4.7, even though there are very few local industries which might be responsible, and it reaches a maximum acidity in the summer, when wind systems from the American north-east reach the island.

Action to solve the acid rain problem is being taken at two levels: reducing the quantity of pollutants being pumped into the atmosphere; and dealing with acid deposition as and when it occurs.

Dealing with the deposition itself can only be a short-term measure. Buildings are sometimes protected from the corrosive action of acid rain by coating them with various chemicals, with some success. More importantly, in Norway and Sweden, scientists have attempted to neutralise their acidified lakes by spraying them with ground-up limestone, or alkali, a process known as liming. This is not easy, because it needs to be carried out frequently – and a sudden change in either the acidity or alkalinity of the water can be a major shock to the ecosystem.

A longer-term solution is pollution control. The technology exists already for limiting emissions from factories, power stations and motor vehicles. However, it is expensive (although not compared to the environmental damage caused by acid rain) and often unpopular politically because it adds to costs of energy production and car manufacture.

Many power stations have switched to low-sulphur grades of coal and are gradually installing various pollution control devices. The filtering system commonly used to reduce emissions of sulphur dioxide is the flue-gas desulphurisation unit, or sulphur scrubber. Unfortunately there is a trade-off with efforts to curb the greenhouse effect, because scrubbers use calcium hydroxide, which is obtained from limestone; carbon dioxide, the main greenhouse gas, is liberated in the process. Scrubbers are not cheap, and environmental protections of this kind is something that many countries claim they cannot afford. However, it has often been suggested that wealthier governments should offer financial help in these cases, if only out of self-interest. Countries in the Eastern bloc would be important targets, because they are still using low-grade coal and antiquated machinery. Action of this kind is also needed in other parts of the world, because of the danger that acid rain will spread as developing countries continue to industrialise.

A milestone in acid rain control came into force in 1987. Appropriately called the 30 per cent Club, it was an agreement signed by many countries which promised to reduce their 1980 sulphur emissions by at least 30 per cent by 1993. A number of members have already cut their emissions by this amount and several others predict cuts by as much as 95 per cent by 1995. For a long time, Britain and the United States (two of the largest emitters) refused to attempt reductions, on the grounds that too little was known about the acid rain problem. However, Britain is bound by a new EEC Directive, which requires it to reduce sulphur dioxide emissions from large combustion plants by 60 per cent by 2003. And the United States now plans to reduce its current emissions by 50 per cent by the year 2000.

Motor vehicle emissions can be cleaned in two ways. The first is the lean-burn engine, which works by adding more oxygen when the fuel is burned. This is still in the early stages of development but does increase fuel efficiency and cuts down on some harmful waste products. However, it is unable to achieve significant reductions in NO_x, particularly at speed.

The second option is a British invention called the three-way catalytic converter, which is fitted to vehicle exhausts. This adds considerably to the cost of a new car but converts 95 per cent of the poisonous fumes to relatively harmless ones. In particular, the nitrogen oxides are converted to nitrogen gas. The main problem is that the carbon monoxide emissions are converted to carbon dioxide, which contributes to the greenhouse effect, so it is a Catch-22 situation. Cars fitted with catalytic converters may also use more fuel.

Catalytic converters are damaged by lead – British cars alone discharge 3,000 tonnes of the stuff every year – so vehicles fitted with them must run on unleaded petrol. (When breathed in, lead damages the brain and central nervous system, especially in children, but it has nothing to do with the acid rain problem.)

Catalytic converters must be fitted by law to all new cars in Japan, the United States and several other countries. They are currently available on few cars in Britain but, from January 1993, new EEC air pollution laws will require all cars to be fitted with them.

In the very long term, alternative fuels are a possibility. Methanol is already being used to power drag racing cars, some vehicles in Brazil run on ethanol (obtained by the fermentation of sugar) and it may even be possible to develop hydrogen (which creates only water as a product of combustion) as the ultimate fuel of the future. But the environmental benefits and costs of these are still unclear.

OZONE

Ozone is a gas, a form of oxygen. It occurs at ground level, where it is man-made but toxic to both animals and plants; and it occurs naturally in the upper atmosphere, where it acts as a shield protecting life on earth from dangerous ultraviolet (UV) radiation.

Ground-level ozone in the air we breathe is produced by a variety of processes. A major source is vehicle exhausts – it is formed when the hydrocarbons combine in sunlight with nitrogen oxides. Ground-level ozone has increased by more than 60 per cent in Europe and North America since the 1950s; the summer of 1989 saw some of the highest levels ever recorded. It creates a photochemical smog, which chokes cities such as Los Angeles, and is potentially even more dangerous than the notorious sulphur smogs of 40 years ago.

But while ground-level ozone is toxic, the thin mist of ozone higher up in the atmosphere is essential to life on earth. Plants and animals depend on it as much as they depend on food and water. It occurs at an altitude of between 16 and 48 kilometres, with a peak concentration in the stratosphere some 20 kilometres above the surface of the earth. Even there, it is so diluted that its concentration is no more than ten parts per million; if it were all brought down to sea level, at atmospheric pressure, it would compress into a layer only 3 millimetres thick.

Although a form of oxygen (it has three atoms in the molecule instead of two), ozone has very different chemical properties which are critical in its role of screening out UV radiation. A certain amount of UV is beneficial; it activates vitamin D in human skin, for example. But too much causes sunburn, skin cancer and eye damage, and may suppress the immune system. It is also believed to slow plant growth and to decrease the productivity of phytoplankton in the sea.

Concern about ozone was first expressed in the early 1970s. Within 15 years, it was clear that the ozone layer had thinned by more than 3 per cent – which was as much as earlier scientific estimates had predicted for the 2020s. The polar regions and higher latitudes have experienced the greatest depletions; in Europe and North America as much as 8 per cent has been destroyed, compared with 'only' 1 per cent at the equator.

But it was a discovery in 1985 which surprised the experts the most – and shocked the world. A team of British scientists reported that they had found a hole in the ozone layer over the Antarctic. Since then, it has grown steadily larger and now covers an area the size of the United States. Meanwhile a new hole, first detected by Canadian scientists early in 1989, had been reported over the Arctic. Both of these are moving around – the Antarctic one has even 'hovered' over Melbourne – and they fluctuate seasonally and according to climatic conditions.

We still do not fully understand the workings of the ozone layer. No one knows what it will be like in as little as five years time, although most experts agree that the rate of depletion is accelerating. The biggest concern is that there may be some more unpleasant surprises in store. Its depletion is potentially so dangerous that it is one of the few global environmental issues that inspires a broad political consensus on the need for action.

How is the ozone layer damaged?
The holes appearing in the ozone layer are man-made. The major culprit responsible is a group of chemicals known as chlorofluorocarbons, or CFCs, although halons (used in some fire extinguishers) are also to blame.

CFCs were invented in 1928. As their name suggests, they are molecules consisting of chlorine, fluorine and carbon atoms. When they are released into the air we breathe they cause no harm at all. They are non-toxic, have no smell and are even non-flammable. Unfortunately, the very same characteristics that render them so inert down here enable them to remain unchanged long enough to drift slowly towards the stratosphere. They make take as long as ten years to reach the ozone layer, which is where they begin to cause serious damage.

When a CFC molecule is exposed to the strong UV radiation high above the earth's surface it is broken apart. This releases a chlorine atom which attacks the ozone. Ozone is a molecule consisting of three separate atoms of oxygen. One of these is pulled away by the chlorine and teams up to form a new molecule called chlorine monoxide. In the process, the ozone molecule has been broken apart. But the destruction does not end there. A free oxygen atom then comes along and takes away the oxygen atom belonging to the chlorine monoxide. This leaves the chlorine alone again, to repeat the process and break apart another ozone molecule. In this way, a single chlorine atom can destroy between 20,000 and 100,000 ozone molecules.

Some 1.2 million tonnes of CFCs are produced every year. They have become an 'essential' ingredient in a myriad of industrial and domestic products. In Europe, as much as half are used as propellents in aerosol sprays. They are also used as refrigerants, in insulation products, as coolants in air-conditioning plants, in cleaning agents (for everything from computer chips to dirty clothes) and in plastic foam packaging for things like the take-away cartons used by many hamburger restaurants. As a consequence, the number of chlorine atoms in the atmosphere has already increased to four or five times the normal level – and continues to increase by about 5 per cent every year.

What are the effects of ozone depletion?

As the ozone layer is depleted, more UV radiation squeezes through the protective shield to reach the earth's surface. An American politician once commented that if too much gets through, we will all have to wear hats and sunglasses, and to apply very strong suntan lotions, whenever we go outside. But the reality is much more frightening.

Research in the US has shown that a depletion of just 1 per cent of the ozone layer causes a 2 per cent increase in the incidence of skin cancers. Worldwide, more than 100,000 people are already dying from predominantly UV-induced skin cancers every year – and the number is rising steadily. More people will also suffer from cataracts and other eye diseases caused by the radiation.

At the same time, a higher dose of UV may slow down plant photosynthesis, the process by which green plants change carbon dioxide and water into carbohydrate and oxygen. Two-thirds of plants tested (mostly crop species) are sensitive to UV radiation in a variety of ways; it reduces leaf size, stunts growth, impairs seed quality and may also increase susceptibility to weeds, pests and disease.

The world's oceans could also be affected. Although very little is known about this, it appears that too much UV radiation tends to disorientate the tiny planktonic creatures in the sea, causing them to die. If this were to happen on a large sale, it would affect the entire ocean ecosystem.

Patching up the ozone holes

If CFC emissions were reduced to zero today, the chemical reactions that are depleting the ozone layer would continue for at least a century. There are two reasons for this: the bulk of CFCs already released have yet to reach the stratosphere; and, once the chlorine atoms have broken away, they will remain active for a very long time. Therefore the effect of any action taken to reduce emissions will not be felt for many years. But this is not a cause for complacency – quite the reverse, it makes the situation all the more urgent.

Unfortunately, the build-up of ground-level ozone (which may give some protection against skin cancer but greatly increases the risk of lung cancer) does not make its own way to the stratosphere; and CFCs will not attack it because they are so inert at ground level. Nevertheless, one idea is literally to patch up the ozone holes by sending our ground-level surplus to the stratosphere, or even by making new ozone high above the earth's surface. The idea is not really feasible, however, mainly because such large quantities would be required.

The obvious answer is to ban the production and use of CFCs. An agreement to do precisely this came into effect on 1 January 1989. Called the Montreal Protocol on Substances that Deplete the Ozone Layer, it is an important first step in galvanising world action to deal with the problem. Fifty countries have now signed the agreement, pledging to reduce the release of certain types of CFCs by 20 per cent by 1994, and by a further 30 per cent by the end of the century. They have also agreed to freeze the production and consumption of halons by 1992.

This is probably the first time in the history of the chemical industry that an important group of compounds is being phased out purely for environmental reasons. But it is not enough to solve the ozone problem. Many experts believe that the Montreal Protocol is far too weak and that a revision, with more drastic reductions, should be negotiated as a matter of urgency. Meanwhile, some countries have already taken it a stage further. The 12 members of the EEC have agreed to go for a total CFC ban by the end of the century. George Bush has also called for a total phase-out in the United States. Incidentally, CFC-driven spray cans have been banned in the States since 1978; this was significant move because some four billion spray cans were sold in the country every year.

Many alternative materials are already available and, to speed up the search, the world's 15 main CFC producers have agreed to carry out toxicity tests jointly. But there are several practical and political hurdles to overcome before it is feasible to reduce worldwide CFC emission to anything approaching zero. The main debate now is what might be acceptable as a suitable substitute. For example, closely-related chemicals called HCFCs (hydrochlorofluorocarbons) are much less damaging to the ozone layer, but not entirely harmless.

There are also several weak links in the chain of international cooperation. Some industrialised countries are convinced of the dangers of ozone depletion but have opted for a gradual phase-out of CFCs to protect their chemical industries. More importantly, many developing countries (which use few CFCs at the moment) consider them essential to their economic growth. For example, China has not signed the Montreal Protocol and plans to put a fridge into every household in the country (which has a population of over one billion) by the end of the century. This will add to worldwide CFC emissions dramatically.

The best solution is for governments of industrialised countries to combine their own efforts, providing subsidies for non-CFC technology, with political pressure in developing countries.

THE GREENHOUSE EFFECT

Temperatures on the moon swing from 100°C during the day to minus 150°C at night. But the earth's temperatures (in the shade) vary only from 0°C to 50°C. How can this be, when the two are both roughly the same distance from the sun?

The answer is simple; the earth has an atmosphere and the moon does not. Certain atmospheric gases regulate the temperature of the earth, maintaining it at a suitable level for life and calming fluctuations between day and night.

We know very little about how this works. But we do know that human activities are tampering with the delicate mix of gases in the atmosphere, with the result that the average global temperature has increased already by some 0.5°C since 1850. This increase has not been steady (there was actually an average temperature decline between 1940 and 1965), but few experts deny that it has happened. There will never be full agreement on something so complex and all-pervading, but seldom has there been such a strong consensus on a major environmental issue. The accumulated evidence leaves little doubt that the world will continue to heat up by between 1.5°C and 4.5°C before the middle of the next century. To put this into perspective, an increase of just 3°C would make it warmer than it has been for 100,000 years.

The problem has been dubbed the 'greenhouse effect' and is considered by many to be the most urgent environmental issue facing the world today. What is most disquieting is that we do not fully understand its likely consequences. A warmer climate, with long summers and milder winters may seem a pleasant prospect but, in the same way that holes have suddenly (and unexpectedly) appeared in the ozone layer, there could be some unpleasant surprises lurking ahead.

What is the greenhouse effect?

A staggering amount of energy enters the atmosphere from the sun. Some bounces back into space, reflected by clouds, but the remainder manages to reach the earth.

Observations from space, however, suggest that the earth radiates so much energy back out into space that its average temperature should be minus 18°C – yet it is more than 30°C warmer. Some of the heat from the sun is being trapped, as if the earth were inside an enormous greenhouse. Indeed, certain gases in the atmosphere have similar properties to the panes of glass in a greenhouse; they are transparent to the sun's rays (which can stream in freely) but allow little heat to escape. This is how the air inside the greenhouse, and the air around the earth, is kept warm. The gases are therefore called greenhouse gases, and their effect, the greenhouse effect. It is a perfectly natural phenomenon.

The term greenhouse effect was first coined in 1863 but, within the last 20 years, it has taken on a new and more ominous meaning. It stands to reason that the greater the concentration of greenhouse gases in the atmosphere, the more of the sun's heat will be trapped and the warmer the world will become. And this is exactly what is happening – because human activities are spewing greenhouse gases into the air at an astonishing rate.

It is particularly alarming to note that the world's six hottest years on record were 1988, 1987, 1983, 1981, 1980 and 1986, in that order. Many scientists are quick to point out that this does not prove anything – that a decade is too short to make any long-term conclusions. Nevertheless, the greenhouse effect itself is not in dispute. Just two questions remain to be answered. How hot will the world become? And what will be the effect?

What are the greenhouse gases?

There are five main greenhouse gases – carbon dioxide, methane, CFCs, ground-level ozone and nitrous oxide.

The most important is carbon dioxide, which causes roughly half the greenhouse effect. Natural carbon dioxide comes from volcanic eruptions, the decomposition of organic matter, gas exchange in the oceans and from respiration by animals. Carbon dioxide makes up only one-thirtieth of 1 per cent of the atmosphere, but it is precisely because this concentration is so small that it can be easily changed by emissions from human activities.

A certain amount of carbon dioxide is absorbed naturally, by 'sinks' or 'sponges' such as oceans, forests and peatlands. But these can no longer cope with the extra 5,600 million tonnes being spewed into the atmosphere artificially every year, by the burning of fossil fuels (such as coal and oil) and forests. The worst offenders are the United States, Western Europe, Japan and the Soviet Union, but industrialised countries as a whole emit several tonnes of carbon dioxide per person per year.

Some very ingenious methods have been developed to measure the atmospheric carbon dioxide levels of the past. Trapped air pockets, inside old telescopes or in glacial ice thousands of years old, are a particularly useful source of information; they show that the greatest change has taken place in the last 150 years, when global levels of carbon dioxide increased by nearly 30 per cent. And they continue to increase by roughly 3 per cent every year.

Methane accounts for 18 per cent of the greenhouse effect, although it is believed to be 20 times more effective in absorbing heat, molecule for molecule, than carbon dioxide. The main natural sources are still not entirely clear, but it is certainly produced by microbes in swamps and marshes, by termites and by wild ruminants. Methane levels in the atmosphere have almost doubled in the last 150 years and are now increasing by just over 1 per cent annually. The main artificial source is agriculture, which produces some 350 million tonnes of methane every year in the guts of cattle and in waterlogged fields such as rice paddies. Unfortunately, the more food being produced, the more methane there is entering the atmosphere.

CFCs account for 14 per cent of the greenhouse effect and are exclusively man-made. Staggeringly, each molecule is several thousand times more effective as a greenhouse gas than each carbon dioxide molecule. Ground-level ozone, produced by the action of sunlight on certain vehicle emissions, accounts for 12 per cent. And nitrous oxide, which is emitted by car exhausts, fossil fuel combustion, nitrogenous fertilisers, ploughing fields and the burning of vegetation, accounts for 6 per cent.

The greenhouse future
If atmospheric concentrations of the greenhouse gases continue to rise, average world temperatures will rise as well. Exactly how this will affect the world no one really knows. One alarming theory is that there could be a sudden and very dramatic change – a kind of

climatic backlash – which, by its very nature, is completely unpredictable.

Most forecasts are based on highly complex mathematical simulations of the world's climate, using advanced computers which were originally developed for long-term weather forecasts. These are far from perfect, for a number of reasons. They do not show enough detail to predict climatic changes in small areas. There are also some major gaps in our understanding of how the global climate works. But most important of all, the models are only as good as the information fed into them – and much of this is unavailable. It is well known that the extent and thickness of ice in the Arctic Ocean, for example, has a profound effect on the workings of the atmosphere, but civilian researchers are denied access to the relevant information, which has been gathered by sonar observations from Soviet and American submarines.

Despite these problems, the scientists and climatologists have considerable confidence in the broad messages of their models. They are certain that the earth is warming at a rate probably never experienced before, and that the greenhouse future will bring some profound changes to the world.

The average temperature of the planet has risen by only 5 degrees since the peak of the last Ice Age – so the effect of any change will undoubtedly be quite dramatic. But this time the speed of change could be as damaging as the change itself, particularly since the ability of the biosphere to adapt is rapidly diminishing as a result of environmental degradation. There is also concern that the temperature increases will be uneven, perhaps ranging from less than 1 degree at the equator to more than 5 degrees at higher latitudes.

Not all the changes will be harmful. Some Soviet scientists believe that the areas available for wheat growing in the Soviet Union will expand, while higher concentrations of carbon dioxide might even improve the yields of certain crop plants such as wheat, soya beans and rice. Ironically, this could give a completely new dimension to the term greenhouse effect.

But while nothing is certain, in many parts of the world the changes are likely to be disastrous. Climatic belts will shift, storms will be more frequent and more severe, monsoon rains will change in reliability and quantity, heatwaves will be longer and hotter, and droughts will be more protracted.

There is intense debate about the effect on sea levels. Some people believe that they could drop. One theory is that, as the world warms up, there will be more snow falling in Antarctica (at the moment it is too cold for it to snow there), which will make the ice sheet grow and sea levels drop. But most experts agree that sea levels will rise. A warmer world may result in the thermal expansion of the oceans, the melting of mountain glaciers in the Alps, the Rockies, the Andes and other mountain ranges, and a major retreat of the polar ice-packs in Greenland and Antarctica. And an increase of 5 degrees would be enough to melt all the permanent Arctic ice. Indeed, research by the Scott Polar Research Institute in Britain has found that the thickness of ice at the North Pole has thinned by up to a third in the last decade.

Sea level rises of up to 1.5 metres by 2050 have been predicted. These would endanger coastal settlements and low-lying cities such as London, New York and Venice. They could flood as much as one-third of all agricultural land worldwide. A large part of Bangladesh could disappear under the Bay of Bengal (making up to 10 million people homeless); just a 50 centimetre rise in sea level would displace 16 per cent of Egypt's population. The President of the Maldives recently expressed grave concern that his country could literally disappear under the sea; its 1,300 tiny islands lie mostly between 1 and 1.5 metres above sea level, and the highest point in the group is only 3.5 metres. The rises might also cause salt to seep into our drinking water supplies.

The effect on wildlife could also be disastrous, largely because the conditions they have evolved to live in will be altering faster than they can adapt. Animals and plants will be unable to exist within their present ranges and will have to colonise new areas; in many cases, particularly where they are surrounded by human developments, this will be impossible. The melting of parts of the Arctic ice sheet would destroy the feeding and pupping areas of polar bears and seals. As the sea level rises, coral reefs will 'drown' under too much water. And many important coastal wetlands, which support fish, shellfish, birds and other animals, would be inundated.

Some of the changes would be quite subtle. The flowering times of tropical trees and other plants would change, preventing synchronisation with their pollinators. The tsetse fly belt in Africa could shift, freeing large marginal areas for unsuitable development. A warmer climate may even make a country such as Britain more liable to invasions of exotic species. And the sex ratios of alligators, sea turtles and some other reptiles could be drastically altered, since the sex of the offspring depends upon the temperature at which the eggs are incubated.

Global warming could itself precipitate further temperature

increases, with a snowballing effect. If the Arctic permafrost melts, for example, it will release billions of tonnes of methane into the atmosphere. Or, if the polar ice-caps melt, less solar energy will be reflected back into space and the earth will automatically absorb more heat.

Solving the greenhouse problem

It is too late to do anything about the vast quantities of greenhouse gases which have been released into the atmosphere so far; we are already committed to a further temperature rise of at least 0.5°C. Therefore it is not a matter of 'How can we stop the climate changing?' but 'How can we slow it down?'

A great deal can be done to reduce further emissions. International action is being taken already to ban the production and use of CFCs (mainly to arrest damage to the ozone layer) and there are several ways of reducing carbon dioxide emissions. More efficient use of energy is the quickest and most effective means, but even a simple switch from coal to natural gas (which has a lower carbon content) would help.

There are also ways of increasing the capacity of the world to absorb excess carbon dioxide by increasing the size of important carbon dioxide sinks, such as forests. Worldwide, there is a considerable net loss of forest every year – so massive tree-planting schemes are essential to reverse this trend. Reducing the demand for firewood (a major drain on forests in the developing world) is another way of redressing the balance; one specific measure would be the widespread introduction of more fuel-efficient methods of cooking, or stoves which use bio-gas or solar energy instead.

The key policy forum for action in the climate-change debate is the Inter-governmental Panel on Climate Change (IPCC). WWF and other conservation organisations would like to see this act as a catalyst for a strong international convention on climate change, with protocols to control emissions of greenhouse gases.

Politicians including Margaret Thatcher, George Bush, Mikhail Gorbachev and Helmut Kohl are beginning to accept that the greenhouse effect must be taken seriously. But many politicians are put off by the enormity and complexity of the problem and, perhaps overawed by the drastic measures necessary to solve it, continue to procrastinate. In addition, many developing countries are unwilling to commit themselves to costly preventative measures that may hinder their development, at least without first seeing major commitment from the industrialised nations.

It is true that the greenhouse effect is a complex issue and cannot be solved in one domain, or in one part of the world. But the projected consequences justify immediate action.

WHAT ARE THE LONG-TERM ALTERNATIVES?

Atmospheric pollution is a byproduct of modern society, and it can be solved in the long term only by dramatic changes in attitude and in the way we live.

One of the best examples is the need to reduce the impact of car traffic on the environment. Unleaded petrol and catalytic converters are essential first steps, but must be accompanied by more fundamental changes in attitude by both governments and individuals. Buying cars with smaller engines is obviously important – in some countries, huge gas guzzlers are becoming as socially unacceptable as fur coats. Car-sharing is also valuable and can reduce the number of cars on the roads quite substantially; in Los Angeles, there are serious financial penalties for employers who fail to organise car-sharing schemes. Low speed restrictions on fast roads can also help by reducing the amount of fuel being used; these have been imposed in the United States ever since the oil crisis (although some states are reverting to faster limits) and now are being considered in other countries for purely environmental reasons.

But most of all, people can be enticed away from their cars by efficient and comfortable (and environment-friendly) public transport systems. In Osaka, Japan, this achieved a drop of two-thirds in its pollution levels between 1970 and 1982. Unfortunately, the current approach in Britain is attempting quite the reverse. British Rail's pricing and timetabling policy is designed to drive people off the trains – simply because the system cannot cope with the demand. Instead of promoting public transport the government recently announced a proposal to spend £12 billion over the next decade on new motorways and roads. As past experience has shown on many occasions, this will encourage even more traffic (and therefore more pollution), at a time when there are 21 million cars on the country's roads already.

The world must become energy-conscious in other ways as well. This requires political will, enlightened economic thinking and personal determination. The less energy each person draws from the national grid, the less power the world consumes and the less pollution there is from power stations.

The ultimate solution, of course, is to find alternative sources of energy that use renewable resources and do minimal harm to the environment.

Is nuclear power a viable alternative?

The nuclear industry has always maintained that nuclear power is a safe alternative to conventional sources of energy. It points to the thousands, maybe millions, killed by lung disease from the air pollution of conventional power stations – and to the thousands of people killed in coalmining accidents. But the word 'nuclear' instantly provokes hysteria in the general public, sometimes with good reason.

Nuclear power generates electricity by tapping the power of the atom, through a controlled process of atomic fission which takes place inside a nuclear reactor. Some 400 nuclear installations provide as much as 17 per cent of the world's electricity needs, and a considerably higher proportion in several industrialised countries. In the United States it provides 18 per cent; in Britain it provides 25 per cent; and in France, which relies on nuclear power more than any other country in the world, it provides no less than 70 per cent.

Some countries are expanding their nuclear programmes. Britain, France and Japan, for example, continue to be committed to nuclear power, while the Soviet Union plans to increase the nuclear contribution to its energy production from 9 per cent to more then 15 per cent by 1993.

But many governments are uncertain about nuclear power, or have halted plans to expand their nuclear programmes. The United States, for example, has not ordered a new plant since 1978. A few have even adopted non-nuclear energy strategies; Sweden currently relies on nuclear power for half its energy requirements but plans to phase it out completely by the year 2010.

Nuclear power has three inherent problems: the health dangers for people working in the industry; difficulties in dealing with its highly radioactive waste; and the inevitable risk of a serious accident.

The fuel used is a silvery-white metal called uranium. This is not an inexhaustible resource, but the quantities required are much smaller than the train-loads of coal and tanker-loads of crude oil that feed conventional power stations.

Uranium is radioactive, and radioactivity is a byproduct of every stage of nuclear power production. Very high doses of radiation are immediately fatal. The effect of low doses appears only after years of exposure, in the form of leukaemia and other cancers. Governments set 'acceptable' levels for workers in the nuclear industry, although many people believe there is no such thing as a 'safe' dose.

Almost everything that comes into contact with the reactor process becomes radioactive, from cooling water and dust to gloves and coats. All reactors leak and minor accidents (involving relatively small releases of radioactive material) occur all the time. At Cumbria's Sellafield nuclear processing plant, in northern England, there have been nearly 300 accidents since it began operating in October 1950.

People working in nuclear installations, or living nearby, are inevitably at risk. Radiation has been blamed for abnormally high levels of childhood leukaemia around Sellafield. A government-commissioned study, published in February 1990, concluded that nuclear workers there were exposed to high levels of radiation (although they were within 'acceptable' limits) and may have unknowingly sentenced their children to death at conception; the radiation is believed to have caused genetic mutations in their sperm, which increased the risk of their children developing the cancer.

The second problem is dealing with radioactive wastes. They cannot be burned – because the smoke would also be radioactive – so they have to be disposed of in other ways, or stored until they are rendered harmless. The problem is that this takes many thousands of years. The most dangerous byproduct of nuclear power production is plutonium, widely considered to be the most toxic substance on earth. It takes 25,000 years for only half of its radioactivity to decay to a safe level (known as its half-life) and can take hundreds of thousands of years longer to decay altogether. Each nuclear reactor produces around 200 kilograms of plutonium every year – enough to inflict cancer on every single person in the world.

Plutonium is classified as high-level radioactive waste. In 1985 the British Government admitted that, by the end of the century, the country will have accumulated more than 4,000 tonnes of waste material in this category, as well as 160,000 tonnes of intermediate waste and over one million tonnes of low-level nuclear waste. Some of it will still be dangerous in 200,000 years time.

For many years most low-level waste produced in Britain and other countries was dumped at sea. But this was later considered too dangerous and, in 1983, an international moratorium on dumping from ships was introduced. It is still being discharged into the sea from the land, although the majority is now buried in shallow graves in the ground. Even so, there are still major contamination problems, and, at a recent conference on North Sea pollution, the British government announced that it is still considering the possibility of burying radioactive material undersea.

There is currently no good way of dealing with high-level radio-active waste, although China and the Soviet Union have offered to take it from other nations for disposal. No suitable stable geological sites have yet been found for burying it deep underground and many people believe that the problem will never be solved satisfactorily.

There is a general phobia about nuclear waste, although people in the industry still claim that the public's fear is exaggerated. A major problem has been called the NIMBY – not in my backyard – syndrome which, interestingly enough, applies to government officials and people in the nuclear industry as well as the nervous general public.

There are several different kinds of nuclear reactor, including advanced gas-cooled reactors, pressurized water reactors and the new (and apparently safer) small integral reactors. But none of them can achieve 100 per cent safety – no technological system can do that. All nuclear installations are built to be as safe as possible but their operation is a delicate balance between too little and too much reactivity and, no matter how many back-up systems there are, there will always be technical malfunctions and human errors. Indeed, one argument is that the more sophisticated the technology becomes, the more room there is for error.

In West Germany, where the nuclear industry is required by law to give details of every episode that affects safety, there were no fewer than 296 accidents in 1988, although they were actually called incidents – the technical term used by the nuclear industry for malfunctions or cock-ups. The details of incidents in Britain and elsewhere are generally unavailable, but there is no reason to believe that the statistics are any better since the technology and operators are of a similar calibre.

However, the nuclear industry has insisted for many years that the chance of a major accident is so remote that it is not worth worrying about. It estimated a 50 per cent chance of such an accident once every 23,000 years. But experience has proved the industry wrong on several occasions and independent studies have put the risk at a more realistic 70 per cent chance once every 5.4 years. Two accidents in particular – at Three Mile Island and Chernobyl – have confirmed the worst nuclear fears and tarnished public perception of the safety of nuclear power.

Three Mile Island is a small island in the middle of the Susquehanna river, in Pennsylvania. Roughly 320 kilometres from New York City, it is the site of a nuclear power station with two pressurised water reactors. On 28 March 1979 several water-coolant feed pumps failed in the second unit and, although the reactor closed itself down within eight seconds, the core temperature began to rise sharply. A series of equipment malfunctions and operator errors allowed the reactor to melt down and radioactive gases poured into the sky.

It was two days before a decision was made to evacuate 3,500 children and pregnant women living within five miles of the plant; another 200,000 people fled the area, unconvinced by official reports that little radioactivity had been released. Many people experienced symptoms of radiation sickness – burning eyes, nausea, diarrhoea, a metallic taste and burning sensations on their skin. Independent studies in the area have also revealed an abnormal number of babies born with serious thyroid problems, a much higher infant mortality, and cancer death rates several times higher than the national average. It is likely that people may still be developing accident-induced cancers for a long time to come. Eleven years after the Three Mile Island accident, more than £700 million had been spent on the clean-up operation. Yet the reactor was still hot – and still contaminated.

The world's worst nuclear accident occurred in the Soviet Union on 26 April 1986. A violation of safety regulations led to two massive explosions in one of the four nuclear power reactors at Chernobyl, a small town some 130 kilometres outside the country's third largest city, Kiev. Radioactive debris was immediately hurled a mile into the sky. Within a few days, a radioactive cloud was hanging over parts of Europe, where levels of radioactivity were higher than they had ever been before. Within two weeks, the radioactivity was being detected throughout the northern hemisphere, from Washington to Tokyo. The fallout was eventually blown to more than 20 countries world-wide.

It took ten days to bring the burning reactor core under control, then a further seven months to enclose it in a massive steel and concrete tomb. Originally 135,000 people and 86,000 cattle had been evacuated from the immediate area around the reactor; three years later another 100,000 people had to be moved because decontamination procedures had not worked. The final death toll is likely to be enormous. Thirty-two people died within a few weeks. But estimates of the total number worldwide who will die as a direct result of the accident range from 1,000 to more than one million. One particular study, sponsored by the United States Department of the Environment, concluded that 12,000 Soviet citizens and 21,000 Europeans will eventually die from Chernobyl-induced cancers.

The total cost is already more than £8 billion. It has been called the most expensive accident in the history of the planet. In Western Europe the radioactive fallout meant that many animals and crops had to be destroyed. The West German government has paid out £150 million in compensation, while sheep farmers in Britain have claimed losses in excess of £10 million. In northern Scandinavia contamination was so severe that thousands of reindeer had to be slaughtered. The full horrors of the disaster are still being assessed. But many experts believe that it could have been several hundred times worse. Chernobyl released only a small proportion of its radio-active material – so no one has been left in any doubt about what could happen if there is a similar accident in the future.

Alternative energy

Electricity production will always be environmentally damaging in one way or another, but some natural sources of energy are cleaner, more efficient and safer than either conventional or nuclear power stations. Harnessing wind, solar, hydroelectric, wave, tidal and geothermal energy has great potential and, although none of these is a perfect alternative, they have two major advantages: they are essentially non-polluting; and they use renewable energy.

Wind is in plentiful supply. But although the efficiency of wind-mills has improved in recent years, it would still take as many as 300 (in an area covering some 200 square kilometres) to produce the same amount of energy as a typical nuclear reactor. These windmill farms are noisy and unsightly (though perhaps not as bad as other power stations) and tend to interfere with TV reception. However, Sweden is considering the replacement of its nuclear reactors with wind turbines anchored to the sea bed, which would solve many of the land-based problems.

Various techniques have been tried to tap the vast resources of the sun. Photo-electric cells, giant mirrors and lenses are used to focus the rays on to towers containing a fluid that conducts the heat to a conventional generator. The basic problem is that it is dark for half the time and, in the other half, the sun does not always shine where it is most needed. But it does work in places like the American south-west, where the sunshine is plentiful and dependable. An alternative to large-scale solar power stations is the use of solar heating in houses. Glass panels on walls and roofs can reduce electricity requirements considerably.

Small-scale hydroelectric schemes may prove to be a valuable source of energy in some areas. But on a large scale they cost a great deal of money and seriously damage the environment. Around the world, there are more than 200 hydroelectric dams that are more than 150 metres tall. Dams have several different purposes: to control river flow; to provide irrigation water; and to generate electricity. But many are built by developing countries for prestige, as a national symbol of development. They ruin habitats, displace large numbers of people (whose homes are flooded) and tend to have limited life-spans.

Wave power has been harnessed with some success, and using a range of applications. The Norwegians have a wave power station at Bergen, which consists of a 20-metre chimney standing in deep water. As the waves rise and fall, air is compressed and used to drive a turbine.

The energy of the ocean tides, as they rise and fall, can be harnessed by damming coastal bays or inlets and building electricity generation stations. There is a successful commercial station on the estuary of the river Rance, near St Malo in northern France. But the number of suitable sites is limited and the constant tidal variations cause major problems. Environmentally, tidal barrages are unpop-ular because they disturb the delicate ecological balance of coastal estuaries.

Geothermal energy is also available only in certain areas, where the conditions are exactly right. Underground, there is a great deal of heat trapped in the earth's molten core and, in some areas, trapped water a few kilometres below the earth's surface absorbs this energy. When steam forms, due to the great temperatures and pressures, it forces the water up and out through fissures or cracks in the earth's crust. Iceland is one of the leading countries in utilising this source of energy; at the beginning of the century Icelandic farmers began to heat their homes with water from hot springs close to the farms, and nowadays 82 per cent of the population lives in houses heated with inexpensive geothermal energy.

There are many other possibilities, particularly on a small scale. The North London Waste Authority, for example, was proposed to supply up to 90 MW to the national grid from its incinerators in Edmonton, thus turning a waste disposal problem into a provider of energy – although there are still air pollution problems with burning waste. But a great deal of work needs to be done before most of these alternative sources of energy can be reasonably expected to produce a substantial amount of power on a world scale. There are political hurdles to overcome as well. The prospect of energy being controlled by the consumers – and of it being plentiful and, ulti-mately, free – does not appeal to the powerful energy lobby.

Climate change caused by excessive carbon dioxide pollution – the greenhouse effect – is seen by WWF as a major threat to species and habitats as well as man. A series of initiatives to widen understanding of the problem may include a workshop in Peking to help the rapidly expanding Chinese nation avoid the mistakes of the West. In Britain, WWF funded the publication of *The Greenhouse Effect and You*, a popular guide showing people how to calculate the greenhouse gases they were causing, and how to reduce them.

In April 1990, WWF hosted 'The Route Ahead', an international conference to raise awareness of the contribution made by road transport to the greenhouse effect, and the measures needed to reduce it.

3 TROPICAL RAINFORESTS

In the 1940s 15 per cent of the earth's land surface was covered in tropical rainforest. Today less than half of it is left. The remainder has been cleared by commercial timber companies, farmers, ranchers and miners – and the cutting, burning and bulldozing continues. It has been called the greatest biological disaster ever perpetrated by the human race.

The total area of rainforest that remains is roughly equal in size to the United States. Restricted mainly to a narrow broken belt straddling the equator, it occurs in three main regions – Latin America, Africa and Asia, although there are also small patches on some Caribbean and Pacific islands, and along the north-east coast of Australia. Brazil has nearly two-fifths of the world's total, and

Zaire and Indonesia each have nearly one-tenth; 54 other countries share the remainder, although most of these have only small patches left.

Vast areas within the forests remain unexplored and have yet to be mapped, let alone studied in detail, but enough is known about them to appreciate their immense value.

- Rainforests are home to more than half the world's animal and plant species and to numerous groups of indigenous peoples.
- The forests are the source of valuable products such as timber, resins, waxes and spices, as well as plant species of outstanding medicinal and agricultural importance.
- They play a critical role in maintaining the heat balance of the earth's surface, and in controlling climatic cycles.
- They hold moisture like a sponge, releasing it slowly to prevent excessive floods and droughts.

There is no easy solution to the rainforest problem. The many underlying political, social, economic, ecological and emotive factors make it a complex issue and the resources of non-governmental organisations such as the WWF are tiny in comparison with those needed to tackle the problem. But the fact remains that the forests continue to be destroyed at such an alarming rate that drastic action needs to be taken within the next few years if they are to be saved.

WHAT IS A RAINFOREST?

There are many different kinds of tropical rainforest although, broadly speaking, they can be divided into three main categories according to their height above sea level.

High on mountain slopes, and usually covered in damp and heavy cloud, are the appropriately-named cloud forests. Their trees are relatively short and widely spaced, leaving a more open forest with a considerable amount of vegetation at ground level. Lower down the mountain slopes are the montane forests and then the lowland forests, the last of which have the greatest diversity of species and are being destroyed the most rapidly.

Seen from a riverbank or road, where light-loving plants form a dense curtain of vegetation, lowland rainforests look virtually impenetrable. But inside they are usually open and easy to walk through. There are well-defined layers providing a range of habitats at different heights above the ground. At the very top, perhaps 50 metres above the forest floor, is the emergent layer. Here the giant trees of the forest thrust through the canopy and spread out well above their neighbours. They enjoy the first share of the sunlight, but have to pay the price of high temperatures, low humidities and strong winds.

Directly below the emergent layer is the canopy itself, a far more hospitable place to live and the site of most animal activity. It acts as an umbrella over all the other layers, intercepting both the sun and the rain, and making the forest beneath dark and steamy. Only about 2 per cent of the sunlight falling on the canopy reaches the jungle floor – tiny flecks of bright light shafting through the gloom, or pale rays of greenish light which have passed through the leaves high above.

A surprising aspect of all rainforests is their soil, which is of very poor quality and infertile. The reason is simple; most of the nutrients in the rainforest ecosystem are locked away within the trees themselves. The reverse is true of the temperate forest ecosystem, which stores its nutrients in the soil.

Despite the similarities in their structure, and in the way they function, geographically separated rainforests are home to different species of animals and plants. For example, gorillas are found only in certain parts of Africa, howler monkeys in certain parts of Latin America and orangutans are found only in a tiny region of Asia. Therefore each time an area of rainforest is destroyed, a unique assemblage of wildlife disappears with it.

There is another, more pertinent, way of categorising tropical rainforests, according to the damage that has been done to them. Untouched virgin areas are called primary forests while those that have been destroyed or damaged (and are gradually recovering) are called secondary forests.

HOW RAPIDLY ARE THE RAINFORESTS DISAPPEARING?

No one really knows how rapidly rainforests are disappearing. Many different estimates have been published but, until quite recently, they have been based largely on informed guesswork.

For a long time it was virtually impossible to measure worldwide forest cover all at once; it would have relied on extensive and coordinated field surveys in dozens of different countries. Nowadays satellite imagery can be used (in conjunction with more conventional sources of information) and the results are generally more accurate and up to date. But it is still very difficult to assess levels of destruction. Should areas that have been damaged by pollution, guerrilla warfare or small development projects be included? Are forests that have been seriously fragmented effectively ruined, or just reduced in size? Should exceptional cases, such as the enormous fire on Kalimantan (the Indonesian part of Borneo) be taken into account? These and many other problems have been tackled in endless different ways, resulting in a wide range of estimates.

The United Nations Food and Agriculture Organisation (FAO) published some figures in 1982 which have been widely quoted ever since; they calculated that up to 100,000 square kilometres of rainforest is cleared completely every year. But two things have changed since those results were published: more information on forest loss has been collected; and the rate of destruction has noticeably increased. So, sadly, more recent estimates paint an even bleaker picture. Many experts now believe that the area being cleared or seriously degraded could be more than twice the FAO figure, equivalent to five times the size of Switzerland every year, or 40 hectares every minute.

The magnitude of the problem is such that, if current rates of destruction continue, most of the world's rainforests will have been cleared completely within the next 50 years, and the few remaining patches will be seriously damaged. The situation is made worse by the fact that most destruction is currently taking place outside the large blocks of rainforest in the Amazon and in Zaire. This means that the surviving remnants in most other countries could disappear during the 1990s or the first decade of the next century.

WHY ARE RAINFORESTS SO IMPORTANT?

Tropical rainforests are home to a greater variety of animals and plants than the whole of the rest of the world. Each species represents a rich, and usually unexplored, reservoir of genes that could be of enormous benefit to medicine, agriculture and industry. As the trees are cut or burned, undiscovered sources of food, cures for cancer and solutions to many other mysteries disappear forever.

In the short term, rainforest destruction threatens the lives of hundreds of millions of people who rely on the forests directly for their livelihoods, or indirectly for watershed management. In the longer term, widespread rainforest loss threatens the global climate and could directly affect people in many other parts of the world.

Artificial forests such as timber plantations could, to an extent, cope with watershed management and some of the other rainforest functions, but they could never replace the rainforests and all their potential benefits to mankind, not least because their biological diversity is virtually zero.

Biological diversity

The variety of wildlife in tropical rainforests is overwhelming. From the highest treetop to the darkest forest floor, the forests are alive with plants and animals – mountain gorillas, toucans, birdwing butterflies, frogs and literally millions of others. The rainforests cover less than 6 per cent of the earth's land surface yet contain more than half of all the species in the world; indeed, some experts have estimated that they contain as many as 90 per cent.

Inside a rainforest it is hard to believe that there is much wildlife there at all. It is common to hear only a few strange sounds and to see virtually nothing. The animals are there, of course, but most are either nocturnal or seldom venture down from their arboreal homes, high in the canopy. Their presence is betrayed only by faint rustlings in the leaves, shrieks and calls or distant crashings through the foliage.

The steamy heat is ideal for many plant species, including brightly-coloured orchids, spectacular climbers and intricate ferns. The constant climate means that there is an ever-growing, ever-green tangle of plant life all year round. There are flowers in bloom at all seasons, attracting bats, birds and insects to their sweet and energy-rich nectar – and there is always a ready supply of leaves and fruit. Even on the gloomy forest floor animals are able to take advantage of this food when it falls down from the canopy above.

The biological diversity of a rainforest is so great that a small patch contains many more species than vast areas in other parts of the world. A century ago the British explorer Henry Bates collected more than 700 different butterflies within just an hour's walk of his home in the eastern Amazon; for comparison, only 60 species occur in the whole of Britain. The Amazon itself harbours 2,000 different fish, ten times as many as in the whole of Europe. And there are more tree species in just 10 hectares of rainforest in Borneo than in the whole of the continental United States.

But many rainforest animals and plants are disappearing even before they have been discovered and identified. This is partly because vast areas are being destroyed before biologists have a chance to explore them properly; 98 per cent of the rich Atlantic coastal rainforest of Brazil has gone, as well as 78 per cent of all the rainforest in the Philippines. We know virtually nothing about what either of these areas contained and therefore have no idea what animals and plants have been lost.

Although the total number of rainforest species is unknown, and is largely a matter for speculation, there is no doubt that it is in the order of many millions. Indeed, the huge jump in species extinctions worldwide projected over the next 50 years is based largely on rates of rainforest destruction.

Medicinal and agricultural importance

Tropical rainforests provide a rich reservoir of genes which can be incorporated, by cross-breeding, into cultivated plants to improve their yields, disease resistance, environmental adaptations and many other factors important to agriculture.

For example, a coffee which is naturally caffeine-free has recently been found surviving in the tiny remnants of forest on the Comoros Islands. Madagascar, next door, has some 50 wild species of coffee and there were probably others which have become extinct, since more than 75 per cent of the country's original forest has been destroyed.

Half a world away, hidden in a tiny patch of cloud forest in Mexico, a wild relative of modern maize has recently been discovered that could revolutionise maize farming in many countries. It appears to be resistant to at least four of the eight major diseases that, until now, maize breeders have been unable to tackle; with the help of cross-breeding, this alone could save an annual loss worth more than US$500 million. But this wild maize also has two other important characteristics: unlike existing varieties of maize, it is a perennial; and it is unique in being adapted to cool and damp conditions. The plant was discovered just in time, as its forest home was threatened with imminent destruction.

It has been estimated that at least 5 per cent of all rainforest plants could also help to solve a wide range of medicinal mysteries. While few have been studied in any detail, many provide important ingredients in modern medicines already, and others have given us substances which can now be made synthetically. Already about 40 per cent of all medicines available on prescription in the United States owe all, or much, of their potency to chemicals from wildlife – largely from rainforest plants.

For example, the US National Cancer Institute has identified more than 1,400 tropical forest plants with the potential to fight cancer. The most famous is the rosy periwinkle, found in Madagascar; it has been used by tribal healers for generations and now supplies vital ingredients for drugs effective against Hodgkin's disease, leukaemia and several other cancers. In 1960 four children out of every five suffering from leukaemia died; but now, largely because of this plant, four out of five survive.

There are almost certainly cures for many other forms of cancer lurking in the rainforests – it is just that we have not yet looked in the right places. Indeed, the rosy periwinkle itself has a close relative which may have its own miracles to offer, although it is a rare plant that is now seriously threatened with extinction.

Human tribes

Rainforest tribes are among the last people on earth to coexist with nature rather than being intent on conquering and destroying it. Cut off from the rest of the world for thousands of years, they have evolved a distinctive and harmonious relationship with the plants and animals around them. They carefully harvest the rich supply of food, medicines and building materials and sometimes clear small patches of forest to grow their own crops. But they make sure that their activities do no lasting harm.

There are more than 1.5 million of these people, scattered throughout the world's rainforests in nearly 1,000 different tribes. And it is inevitable that some are still unknown to the rest of mankind. But their numbers have declined rapidly since their rainforest homes have been invaded by the 'civilised' world. Some indigenous peoples, such as the Kuna Indians of Panama, appear to have adapted well to modern society, while conserving their traditions. Others have been able to retreat to remote and isolated corners of the forests where, temporarily, they are safe. But most groups have been unable to adapt to the onslaught.

When Christopher Columbus sailed for the Americas in the late 15th century there were between six and nine million Indians living in the Amazon forest. According to the World Bank no more than 5 per cent of this population has survived. Their people have been poisoned, bombed and gunned-down – even during the last 20 years – by ruthless land-hungry invaders. Diseases to which they have no immunity, such as influenza, measles and smallpox, were deliberately introduced into their villages. They were considered to be savages, with 'ridiculous' customs and superstitions – and, above all, with no feelings and no rights.

The largest remaining group of South American Indians is the Yanomami, living deep in the Amazonian forest. They are so aggressive to outsiders and other tribes that they have been dubbed the 'fierce people', yet even they have suffered the ravages of these western-style invasions. There are 21,000 Yanomami people in the Amazon. Like most forest inhabitants, their natural lifespan is about 40 years. They usually die from diseases easily cured by modern medicines but, at the same time, may have developed some of their own remedies (with the help of rainforest plants) which could benefit people in other parts of the world. In particular, they make no clear distinction between mental and physical illness, and as such may hold the key to new treatments for conditions such as schizophrenia and severe depression.

Forest tribes were generally regarded as forest animals – no one really cared whether or not they survived. Nowadays, in most places, they are officially regarded as citizens, with rights like anyone else, but these rights are rarely recognised in practice. Politicians and others determined to destroy their forests are still inclined to dismiss any opposition from tribal people as a 'nuisance' or simply as 'emotional'.

Many other people traditionally live in or around tropical rainforests. They do not belong to tribal groups, but their communities have relied on the forests for all their raw materials for hundreds of years. In total, there are believed to be 140 million non-tribal people relying exclusively on tropical rainforests for their survival.

Rainforest products
Rainforests are the source of many valuable products other than timber – fruit, latex, oils, cocoa, vanilla, spices and rattan among them. One of the best of these products is fruit, simply because removing a large part of the harvest does not damage the forest. But others can be more valuable; the international trade in rattan is already worth more than US$1.5 billion every year.

People all over the world take many rainforest products for granted – even farmyard chickens came originally from the forests of Asia. But considering the impact many of these have already had on our lives, there could be some very exciting discoveries in the future.

The potential value of these alternative products is well illustrated by the results of a study near Iquitos, in Peru. It was discovered that an incredible US$6,820 could be earned every year from 1 hectare of rainforest by harvesting its natural resources on a sustainable basis. In contrast, extracting all the marketable timber in a single operation earned a once-only income of just US$1,000. These figures were based on local market prices; if there was sufficient demand abroad, the value could be even higher.

Indonesia has been developing its non-timber products for export for several years. They were valued at US$28 million in 1973 and increased to some US$200 million in 1982. In the same two years, exported timber products earned the country US$583 million and US$899 million respectively.

Environmental services

There is a popular misconception that rainforests are the 'lungs of the world'. But scientists now believe that their effect is neutral; they absorb as much oxygen through the decay of organic matter as they produce through photosynthesis. However, they do have a significant effect on other local and global systems.

For a start rainforests play a particularly important role in soil protection and watershed management. As their name suggests, they receive an enormous amount of rainfall. By breaking the impact of severe tropical storms, they protect fragile soils and, at the same time, hold the water like a sponge, releasing it slowly and steadily. When rainforests are removed, soil erosion becomes a terrible problem, and torrential rainstorms cause serious flooding, while dry periods lead to drought. For example, a small 7,500-hectare cloud forest reserve above the Honduran capital of Tegucigalpa, in Central America, protects a watershed which provides 40 per cent of the city's drinking water. If the reserve were to disappear, and water had to be provided from another source, the extra costs involved would be at least US$100 million.

Many experts believe that there is a direct link between the extent of rainforest cover and local (and even global) rainfall patterns. Studies in Amazonia suggest that more than 50 per cent of the rain remains within the forest ecosystem. It is constantly being transferred by the trees into the atmosphere, where it collects in storm clouds, to be rained back down again. Removal of the forest could reduce the moisture reaching the atmosphere, leading to a significant decline in rainfall. In fact, there are several examples from the tropics linking deforestation with drought conditions soon afterwards.

The overall role of tropical forests in the global climate has long been a subject of speculation. It is likely that their destruction on a massive scale could change climatic patterns all over the world, although no one knows precisely what the effects could be.

Since rainforests are relatively dark, they absorb heat. But when they have been chopped or burned down they are replaced with crops or grass, which are much lighter and reflect more of the sun's energy. This may already be causing a change in weather patterns thousands of miles away.

Rainforests are also involved in the carbon cycle which, ultimately, affects global warming. Living trees soak up carbon dioxide from the atmosphere and store large quantities of carbon. When they are destroyed, most of this escapes, either immediately if they are burned, or within a few years due to biological decay. The carbon is oxidised and returns to the atmosphere as carbon dioxide, which is the principal global warming gas. Some estimates suggest that the burning of tropical rainforests may contribute anything up to 20 per cent of the human-induced emissions of carbon dioxide, making it the second biggest source after fossil fuel combustion. Methane and nitrous oxide, two more greenhouse gases, are also released by rainforest destruction.

Some logging companies have claimed that timber extraction is a far better way of using the rainforests because it has a lesser effect on global warming. But this is not true. Vast amounts of forest are destroyed when they remove the target trees; much wastage occurs in the processing; the logging and processing machinery burns fossil fuels; and the roads they build are a major factor in encouraging the burning and settlement of new forest areas.

HOW ARE RAINFORESTS BEING DESTROYED?

The trouble with rainforest destruction is that it is hard to point a critical finger at a single identifiable villain. Rhino poaching has poachers and whaling has whalers, but rainforest destruction has a motley collection of commercial loggers, cattle ranchers, cash-croppers, industrialists, landless peasants and even governments and aid agencies, all involved in varying degrees in different parts of the world. More importantly, many of the people destroying rainforests can hardly be called villains. The landless peasants, desperate for a patch on which to grow their food, are really the victims of other, underlying, problems such as overpopulation and widespread poverty.

Commercial logging

The timber industry is directly responsible for as much as 40 per cent of rainforest destruction, with the worst affected areas being in west Africa and south-east Asia. Having exploited most of the forests in these regions, the industry is now shifting its attentions to the forests of central Africa and Amazonia. After that, there will be nowhere else to go.

Tropical timber exports are worth more than US$8 billion a year and, since they are central to the economies of many developing countries, few governments are going to stand in the industry's way.

Japan is the largest consumer, accounting for roughly one-third of the total market, with the European Community coming a close second. Worldwide demand is growing fast and exporting governments naturally want to make as much money as they can as quickly as they can. But the pressure to reap the rich short-term rewards on offer encourages speed, which has become the top priority, rather than careful management. Nowadays, a giant tree that once took several men a whole day to hack down with axes can be felled by a single man armed with a chainsaw in about 10 minutes. And it is a terribly wasteful business. The traders are interested only in the wood that is easiest to sell, such as mahogany, ebony and rosewood. They cut perhaps only one tree out of every 20 in the forest and, in the process, damage most of the others with their heavy equipment.

But logging has far wider ramifications. By building roads and installing services, the timber companies open up previously inaccessible areas of rainforest for colonisation. There is then an influx of new settlers, who clear even larger areas for their crops, in the shadow of most logging operations. On this basis, the FAO has estimated that the total rainforest loss caused directly or indirectly by logging is nearer 70 per cent.

Farming to survive

Millions of poor people are forced to destroy tropical rainforests simply to survive. Whenever land is cleared, for whatever reason, they are ready to move in and start farming. In some countries, often with the help of unfulfillable promises, they have been actively encouraged to do so in order to defuse pressure for land elsewhere. But usually they are forced away from their own homes by wealthy landowners, massive development projects, population pressures or poverty – they have no choice but to clear forest areas to provide themselves with land on which to live. So they burn the forests and plant their crops, but the infertile soils become thoroughly exhausted within just two or three years and, to keep producing food for their families, the farmers have to abandon the land and clear another patch of forest.

In Laos this slash-and-burn clearance is destroying up to 3,000 square kilometres of rainforest every year; if this rate continues unchecked there will be no forest left in the country by 2030. Slash and burn is the major cause of destruction in most threatened rainforests, but it would be unnecessary if good agricultural land could be shared more fairly, instead of being held by the wealthy minority.

Cattle ranching

Cattle ranching has rightly earned itself a reputation for turning rainforests into hamburgers. At the same time, it turns the most productive ecosystem in the world into the most barren. It creates few jobs and only short-term profits.

Beef cattle are the main destroyers of rainforests in Central America and have caused the clearance of large areas in Amazonia. The vast herds are grazed not to feed local people but to provide cheap beef for export – mainly for burgers in fast-food chains. When the forests are cleared to make space for planting grass the timber is completely wasted. In Amazonia, cattle ranchers have destroyed timber worth some US$8 billion, which is more than commercial logging in the region has earned.

However the pastures that are created in this way survive a maximum of ten years, by which time the grazing potential has decreased from seven head of cattle per hectare to just one per hectare. Eventually, overgrazing and torrential rains turn the land into semi-desert and the ranchers move on to another patch of forest.

Ninety per cent of the beef exports during the last 25 years have gone to the United States. The American fast-food industry alone is thought to have been responsible for the destruction of more than a quarter of Central America's magnificent rainforests. According to some reports, 5 square metres of rainforest have to be cleared to produce enough grazing land for one hamburger. The biggest importers in the US now claim that they do not use rainforest beef, although some does still find its way into the country, and the beef barons are seeking new buyers.

In Brazil the destruction is not even necessary. There is an area of unused farmland the size of Chile, with better soil, in the south of the country. Forest clearance is merely cheaper, especially with the help of a US$2 billion investment by the government to provide tax breaks and other indirect incentives.

THE AMAZON BASIN

Early explorers were so impressed by the size of the Amazon they called it the Ocean River. The second longest river in the world, after the Nile, it flows for about 6,440 kilometres (as far as from London to New Delhi) from its source in the snow-capped Peruvian Andes to its delta on the Atlantic Ocean in northern Brazil. It drains an area the size of Australia which contains the largest remaining tropical rainforest anywhere on earth. This luxuriant wilderness covers two-thirds of South America, north and south of the equator. Most of the forest is in Brazil, but there are parts in eight other South American countries – Peru, Ecuador, Bolivia, Colombia, Venezuela, Guyana, Surinam and French Guiana.

The Amazon itself is an extraordinary river. It has about 15,000 tributaries, four of which are more than 1,600 kilometres long; it pours water into the Atlantic Ocean with such volume and force that 160 kilometres offshore a sailor can reach down to the sea and scoop up a glass of freshwater; at the river's mouth its north and south banks are farther apart than Paris and London; and, 50 kilometres upstream, it is still wider than the English Channel.

Contrary to popular belief, this ancient habitat is not particularly stable. Recent evidence shows that during the last 100,000 years the climate and the vegetation of the Amazon have experienced some dramatic changes. This is in relatively recent geological times. It seems that glaciations in polar and mid-latitudes were periods when the Amazonian climate was cooler and drier. Just 18,000 years ago, when much of Britain was beneath ice, the Amazon rainforest was reduced to small islands surrounded by savanna grasslands. These islands have been called 'refugia' by biologists – they were refuges where rainforest species survived.

The wildlife in the Amazonian forest today forms a biological treasure trove, containing more than a tenth of all the world's animal and plant species – 100 square metres of forest can contain as many as 230 different trees, compared to a typical temperate forest which has a mere 10 to 15. And there are more than 2,500 species of trees in the Amazon altogether.

The region is also home to a number of groups of tribal Indians and to the *caboclos*, who are long-standing settlers with a mixture of Indian and foreign blood. The settlers are rubber-tappers, supplementing their incomes by gathering Brazil nuts. They have received a great deal of international publicity recently because of their fight to stay in their rainforest homes. When Chico Mendes, president of the rubber-tappers' union in the Brazilian state of Acre, was murdered in 1988, their plight was publicised all over the world. Mendes had challenged the cattle ranchers who were cutting down the forests where his members worked.

Cattle ranching is just one of many threats to the Amazon rainforest, the other main ones being colonisation programmes, road projects, logging, mining and hydroelectric dams. In the past 40 years, the many Amazonian states have been intent on exploiting its vast natural wealth and on opening up the forest to new settlers – an area of primary rainforest the size of Belgium went up in smoke in 1988 alone.

For example, there are plans to build 125 hydroelectric dams in the Brazilian Amazon over the next 20 years, with the help of US$500 million in loans from the World Bank. Another project funded largely by the World Bank is the Polonoreste road in Rondônia, Brazil. As the road progresses through the forest, more and more landless farmers from Brazil's impoverished and overpopulated south-east arrive to cut down the newly-accessible trees, which then allows them to plant their crops. In 1960 Rondônia's population was 10,000, mostly Indians; by 1985 it had grown to more than one million.

The Amazon also has tremendous mineral wealth, including the richest deposits of iron ore on earth, as well as gold, diamonds, uranium, titanium and tin. Brazil alone earns some US$9 billion a year from mining operations. In recent years there have been several major gold rushes, fuelled by recession and widespread unemployment, so that there are now more than one million gold prospectors in the region – mostly employees of large companies using heavy machinery rather than old-fashioned gold miners panning by hand. In 1988 they took about 83 tonnes of gold out of the Amazon. They are disrupting the lifestyles of indigenous forest people (some 45,000 gold miners now occupy Yanomami tribal lands), clearing airstrips, cutting access roads in the jungle and polluting the rivers with mercury. Thousands of tonnes of mercury, which is illegal but which is still widely used in the separation process, have already been discharged into the Amazon and its tributaries.

In November 1989 the Brazilian president promised to safeguard the Indians' interests, but then allowed the gold miners to stay, as long as they vacated Indian reserves. Since there is no proper demarcation of these reserves, the ruling is unenforceable.

Indeed, the Brazilian government actively encourages the colonisation, industrialisation and destruction of the Amazon. One of the worst examples is the massive *Grande Carajas* programme in the north-east of the country. This horrendous scheme will affect one-sixth of Brazilian Amazonia and includes a variety of new mines, plantations, ranches and heavy industries. More than 6,000 square kilometres of forest will be cleared every year just to provide charcoal for a single aluminium smelter. One of the main projects is an open-cast iron ore mine which will be the largest in the world, financed with the help of a US$600 million loan from the European

Community. It requires a new 900-kilometre railroad linked to a new port being built at São Luis, both of which are being funded by the World Bank. Power for the mine will be provided by a series of new dams; the first of these is finished and has flooded over 2,000 square kilometres of forest. There are plenty of incentives for companies to join this project, including a tax-free status for up to ten years and less stringent pollution controls than elsewhere in the country. The overall aim is appalling: specifically to open up a large section of the Amazon to industry and agriculture.

SAVING THE WORLD'S RAINFORESTS

Why have so many attempts to save the world's tropical rainforests failed?

For a start, a lack of resources has not helped. But the main reason is that the underlying causes of rainforest destruction have been largely ignored. In the past it was widely believed that the problem could be tackled simply by establishing an extensive network of protected areas, and keeping people out. But while national parks and reserves will always play an important role in rainforest conservation, most of them are poorly protected and exist only on paper; they cannot be expected to solve the rainforest problem alone.

From a purely practical point of view, complete protection on such a grand scale could never be enforced. In the Brazilian state of Rondônia 140 poorly paid men from the federal and military police are expected to turn down large bribes while attempting to guard an area as large as West Germany. As you might expect, the system simply does not work. There are too many people traditionally relying on the forests for their survival, and too many economic pressures encouraging governments to exploit the same forests for short-term gain.

Logging in all but nine of the 73 provinces in the Philippines was officially banned early in 1989. But a multi-million-dollar industry was at stake and anti-logging campaigners began to receive death threats; at least two of them have been murdered. Even before the ban most logging operations in the country violated one law or another; twice as many Philippine logs were being smuggled into Japan as were imported legally.

Hiding a sufficient area of rainforest away from the onslaught of loggers, farmers, ranchers and miners is therefore unrealistic, a dream that will never come true. And in some cases, it is even unnecessary.

Instead, people have to be given a vested interest in conservation. Paradoxically, it follows that finding ways to exploit rainforests – without threatening their long-term future – is ultimately the best way of saving them. This is the basis of today's enlightened approach by WWF and many other conservation organisations. It is the lesser of two evils, but clearly preferable to the option of total destruction. It has not been an easy concept to sell to a general public more interested, perhaps understandably, in protecting wildlife than in businessmen and politicians. But ironically the real obstacle in many countries is proving to be a lack of political will.

Protected areas

Some 4.5 per cent of the world's rainforests are within protected areas. WWF would like to see this figure more than doubled by the end of the century. One suggestion is to establish a network of 500 parks and reserves, representing all the major rainforest eco-systems on each continent. The aim would be for half of them to be totally protected and the other half to be exploited on a sustainable basis.

But this is not as straightforward as it sounds. Which are the most critical areas to protect? How large should they be? How can they be most effectively managed? Where is the money going to come from? These are important questions to ask, and there are no simple answers. Fortunately, some countries, such as Cameroon and Costa Rica (which has set aside over 20 per cent of its territory for protection) are far-sighted enough to take action before the experts have all the necessary information at their fingertips.

Another important recent development is the idea of debt-swapping or debt-for-nature agreements. Most major banks in the industrialised world are owed large amounts of hard currency by some 20 developing nations, and it appears increasingly unlikely that these debts will ever be repaid in full. So WWF and other conservation groups have begun to pay off small proportions of them (at reduced prices) in return for rainforest protection.

The first such deal was signed with Bolivia, South America's most impoverished country, on 12 July 1987. In exchange for a reduction of US$650,000 (purchased for just US$100,000 by Conservation International, a non-profit environmental group in the United States) from its crippling US$4 billion foreign debt, Bolivia agreed to conserve 1.6 million hectares of its rapidly diminishing forests. Unfortunately the deal was criticised because none of the local Indian communities were either consulted or considered. And many

Bolivians mistakenly believed that the government had actually sold off part of the country.

Suspicion surrounding the debt-swapping idea has been a major factor in preventing similar deals in neighbouring Brazil which could, in theory, exchange some of its enormous foreign debt (currently standing at US$112 billion) for agreements to preserve the Amazon.

The Tropical Forestry Action Plan

The Tropical Forestry Action Plan (TFAP) is a collaborative venture between the World Bank and the United Nations designed to raise the level of development spending in tropical rainforest areas. It was launched in 1987 with a five-year budget of over US$8 billion. However, although it is barely beyond the planning stage, the TFAP has already been extensively criticised by conservationists. All the indications are that its whole concept is wrong, and it could prove to be extremely dangerous if its aid money is misused.

Conservation groups believe that the TFAP has potential only if all its projects are based on the conservation and sustainable use of rainforest areas. Initially, it could help by stopping aid agencies funding development projects which lead to rainforest destruction, but this would require full and open environmental impact assessments before any financial decisions are made. However, only 8 per cent of the TFAP budget has been allocated to ecosystem conservation. The remainder is destined for industrial use, forestry plantations and bureaucracy.

Another major criticism is that the TFAP shifts the blame for deforestation to landless peasants, belittling the major destructive role played by massive development projects such as hydroelectric dams and roads, many of which are funded by the World Bank. The TFAP is also biased against the opinions, needs and rights of traditional forest peoples. It is a top-down process, in which local communities are not consulted, when in fact they should be consulted extensively.

The aid agencies involved in the TFAP have indicated that they may be willing to respond flexibly to these concerns, but the entire process requires a fundamental revision if it is to tackle rainforest destruction rather than accentuate the problem. It was to the TFAP that the British government committed £100 million in 1989, when it was applauded in the press for pledging the money 'to save the world's rainforests'.

The International Tropical Timber Agreement

In contrast to the TFAP, the International Tropical Timber Agreement (ITTA) is widely considered to be the best hope of gaining government cooperation in efforts to save the world's rainforests. A unique agreement designed to control worldwide trade in tropical timber, it came into force in 1985 after eight years of negotiations.

The ITTA was established under the United Nations Conference on Trade and Development (UNCTAD) International Commodities Agreements System. Each agreement within the system is designed to allow regulation of the world market in a particular commodity. What makes the ITTA so special is the fact that it is the first to recognise the importance of conservation.

ITTA is primarily a trade agreement seeking to improve and rationalise the market conditions for tropical hardwood trading. But the preamble of the ITTA recognises:

> the importance of, and the need for, proper and effective conservation and development of tropical timber forests with a view to ensuring their optimum utilisation while maintaining the ecological balance of the regions concerned and of the biosphere.

In order to carry out its objectives the ITTA created in 1986 the International Tropical Timber Organisation (ITTO) with a secretariat based in Yokohama, Japan. ITTO now has over 40 members which, between them, account for around 75 per cent of the world's rainforests and 95 per cent of the tropical timber trade. Despite initial opposition from several governments, it firmly incorporates the idea that sustainable management must be a part of future tropical forestry. Partly as a result of pressure from conservation groups, nowadays it actually states its mission as being primarily to promote rainforest conservation.

In fact ITTO's key role is to strike a balance between utilisation and conservation of rainforest resources. This is being tackled in a variety of different ways:

- By developing demonstration models, to show how timber production can be sustained.
- By encouraging the development of suitable national rainforest policies.
- By establishing better rules and standards for the timber market.
- By improving cooperation and coordination between producer and consumer countries.

Ideally suited to these tasks, ITTO is the only international forum for bringing together timber traders and delegates from most of the countries involved to discuss the exploitation of tropical timber. Non-governmental organisations such as WWF are given observer status at its various meetings.

WWF believes that the entire tropical timber trade should be based on sustainable utilisation of rainforests by the mid-1990s. This would require a major shift in forestry policy because, according to ITTO itself, only one-eighth of 1 per cent is currently managed for timber production without irreversible damage.

Commercial logging is, of itself, impossible without causing some damage to the forest, no matter how carefully it is done. But the world is driven by economic values and, consequently, harvesting the timber is widely considered to be the only option for rainforest protection outside national parks and reserves. ITTO's success in fulfilling its role therefore depends on the will and financial commitment of the government members. It has already financed over £8 million worth of projects, three-quarters of which are directly concerned with conservation and sustainable management. And at a recent ITTO meeting, considerable progress was made when governments called on the timber traders to play a more supportive role. At the same meeting, the International Timber Trade Federation supported the idea of a tax on European timber imports to help fund ITTO's activities.

But its members still lack a sense of urgency and, in reality, pitifully few countries are making a serious attempt at rainforest conservation. However Thailand proved itself an exception in January 1989 by cancelling all its logging concessions – its rainforest cover had been reduced from 70 per cent to less than 18 per cent in the previous 40 years. But the logging ban came after a series of mudslides and floods in November 1988 which were blamed on deforestation and claimed the lives of 430 people.

Four days after the Thai ban became law the agriculture minister of Thailand cancelled 276 logging concessions, covering about 30 per cent of the country; timber companies were ordered to stop all logging immediately and to remove their equipment from the forests. The immediate financial loss to the Thai government was enormous – £12 million per year in royalties, plus an unknown amount in compensation to timber companies and the 200,000 workers who lost their jobs. And enforcement of the logging ban was also expensive. But the sad fact was that Thailand's logging problems were simply exported to neighbouring countries.

Thailand itself immediately began seeking alternative sources of raw timber. Within two days Laos had been persuaded to drop its own ban on raw timber exports to meet the new demand. Burma was also tempted and, desperate for foreign trade, threatened its huge teak forests with an agreement to provide a major proportion of Thailand's raw wood requirements. In an effort to encourage timber imports, the Thai government reduced the import tax on logs from 7 per cent to just 1 per cent.

Governments may be characteristically slow in waking up to the environmental consequences of their actions, but the timber trade itself has shown a general lack of support for much of ITTO's work. Indeed, some environmental groups believe that ITTO's voting rights are biased in the trade's favour and that this has, in some cases, hampered progress. Certainly, ITTO's activities so far have been insignificant compared to the scale of the problem.

Ultimately, of course, if all the world's rainforests are destroyed, so is the lucrative tropical timber trade, and this is a fact that increasingly worries the timber companies. But so far they have shown a marked lack of interest in sustainable logging. A major problem is that there is no incentive to look after specific areas of land. The timber companies are generally given short logging concessions of only five or ten years and, since tropical hardwoods grow slowly, it makes business sense for them to take out as much of the best wood as possible and then to get out themselves. If they were given longer concessions of, say, 60 to 100 years, they would be more selective in their logging operations. And to protect their long-term interests, they would have to keep small-scale farmers off the land to give the forest sufficient chance to recover.

Another solution is to leave a substantial core area in the middle of each forest completely untouched. There is evidence to suggest that animals and plants which take refuge in these unlogged pockets are then able to spread out gradually after the loggers have gone and the forests have begun to regenerate. But again, this will work only if the regenerating areas can be protected from the inevitable invasion of small-scale farmers.

The ideal solution is to balance logging with the needs of indigenous people, who could exploit the same forests (also on a sustainable basis) for non-timber products. One of ITTO's current field projects is to study this possibility in the Brazilian state of Acre, in the hope of demonstrating how loggers and indigenous people can coexist.

Consumer power

Governments of many countries in the tropics, perhaps understandably, resent the incessant moralising about their rainforests from rich temperate nations, especially as they have seen those same rich nations damage their own environments, and those of others, in order to get so rich. But it is possible to tip the balance in favour of conservation, in an entirely different way – with the help of consumer power.

For example, consumer power can strongly favour timber which has come from sustainably managed forests. There is some evidence to suggest that people in many consumer countries would be willing to pay considerably more for wood if they were sure that it had not resulted in irreversible forest destruction. This alone could encourage the governments concerned to take an interest in conservation.

Consumer power can also increase the demand for non-timber rainforest products such as resins, oils, fibres and fruits. This will encourage the development and careful management of extractive reserves which integrate conservation with the needs and chosen lifestyles of local communities, and cause virtually no disruption to the ecosystem. A good example of an extractive reserve is Korup in south-west Cameroon, where WWF, with government backing, is seeking to give local tribesmen a vested interest in halting forest destruction. The tribesmen are directly involved already in a systematic search for useful plants with medicinal properties, the harvesting of fruit and nuts, fish farming and the development of natural products such as honey.

One of the challenges for extractive reserves is to develop traditional and new rainforest products that have a reasonable market price in the industrialised world, not just in local markets. As an example, an ice-cream manufacturer in the United States has just launched a new flavour called 'Rainforest Crunch', made with Brazil nuts and cashew nuts collected by people living in the Amazon. Albeit in a small way, this is encouraging the forests to be used for their natural harvest. Several cosmetics firms are also involved in extractive forest products.

There is still some scepticism about this sort of product development, particularly among the larger companies, but a number of smaller ones are very keen on the idea. And with so many consumers taking a direct interest in rainforest conservation, it is beneficial for companies to be able to advertise their involvement through these innovative products.

Ultimately, of course, a complete boycott of tropical timber, and other products originating from countries that do not attempt to preserve their forests, may be necessary. Just the threat of a boycott has aroused an uncharacteristic interest among timber traders in international initiatives to save rainforests. But whether this is due to a fear of strong feelings among consumers, or in recognition of the need to protect the world's rainforests and therefore the trade's future supply of timber, is open to debate.

Saving the world's remaining tropical forests is WWF's main international conservation priority. More than half the world's known species live in them, and there is increasing awareness that forests play a vital role in controlling atmospheric pollution. Round the world, WWF has 161 tropical forest conservation projects.

Logging is a principal cause of forest destruction. WWF-UK is campaigning to persuade the UK government and timber trade that by 1995 only logs from sustainably managed sources should be allowed into Britain.

4 DROUGHT AND FAMINE

Distressing pictures of starving children and weeping mothers, reduced to scratching in the dust for grains of millet or living in makeshift camps in the middle of deserts ravaged by drought, have shocked the world in recent years. But these images have become dangerously clichéd. They imply that famine is a natural disaster caused by drought. This is misleading. Drought does result in crop failures, loss of livestock and hardships – it has done so many times in the past – but it does not always result in famine. Instead, drought reveals and compounds a complexity of underlying political, social, economic and ecological problems that together cause famine.

Unfortunately it is the drama of hungry people that makes the headlines, rarely the real issues behind the scenes of starvation. The causes of famine are too drawn-out and less dramatic than the effects, so we are not made sufficiently aware of what is really happening in so many parts of the world. Therefore our charity is concentrated on relieving the current symptoms; our instant response is a flood of food aid.

There is no doubt that food aid and other forms of disaster relief are essential to tide the hungry over an immediate crisis and to provide them with shelter, clothing and medical supplies. It does save lives; but it is not the best way of alleviating human suffering. Indeed, its effect is often cosmetic; it is like sticking a bucket under a leaky roof, but never fixing the roof itself. Unless more efforts are put into ameliorating the underlying causes of famine, then we are doing little to avert future repetitions of past disasters.

WHAT CAUSES FAMINE?

A famine is an extreme shortage of food over a long period of time. It can be caused by a variety of things, including crop disease, pest infestations, the need to abandon farmland because of war, or bad weather.

There is a tendency to think of it as a modern phenomenon. But famine has been recorded in many parts of the world for thousands of years. The Bible contains numerous references to times when crops failed, and there are many more recent examples, such as the notorious potato blight that devastated Ireland in the mid-19th century.

But while famine may not be new, it has changed. Modern famines do not affect the rich, developed world: they affect poor people in poor countries. The problem is most acute in a region of Africa called the Sahel, a transient band of countries on the southern fringes of the Sahara Desert, from Mauritania in the west to Ethiopia in the east, which appears to be experiencing more frequent and longer droughts – and famines – than usual.

Is famine an act of God?

Droughts are a common and normal aspect of life in the Sahel. Meteorologists have been recording rainfall across much of the region for less than 100 years, but there are indications of past droughts in the 1680s, 1740s and 1750s, and the 1820s and 1830s; during this century, drought has been experienced between 1910 and 1920, again in the 1940s, and most recently in the 1970s and 1980s. The extended duration of the latest drought, and the evidence from longer-term records, have tempted some scientists to suggest that the Sahel is experiencing an actual change in climate; for example, records from Sudan reveal a drop of about 15 per cent in annual rainfall during the last 70 years.

But climate change has been a contentious issue for some time. One of the reasons is that the precise mechanism driving the drought machine is not fully understood. It appears that when the jet-stream circulation of air over Europe is weak, it holds back the northward movement of the monsoon rains in Africa. There also appears to be a strong relationship between rainfall in the Sahel and changes in the surface temperature of the tropical parts of the Atlantic Ocean. This is not as absurd as it sounds; much of the rain in the Sahel originates from evaporation at the ocean surface, which is very slow if the waters are cool. Years of poor rainfall are linked to years when the equatorial Atlantic surface waters are cooler than usual, although exactly why there are these changes in temperature is still to be resolved.

But there are a number of theories which attempt to explain the changes we appear to have been witnessing in recent years. One is the idea that the climate in the Sahel has been getting progressively drier since the end of the last great Ice Age; another proposes that industrialisation in the northern hemisphere is causing the climate of the Sahel to dry up. Human misuse of the land may even be to blame; land without vegetation reflects solar energy back into space and gives less moisture to the air, so rain clouds do not form; and soil dust, blown into the atmosphere by the scorching desert winds, makes it more difficult for air to rise, again preventing rain-cloud formation. Less rain means less vegetation, and the cycle continues.

But there is little conclusive evidence to support these notions. Indeed, not all meteorologists are convinced by the idea of permanent change, and some now believe that the present lack of rainfall in the Sahel is not abnormal. The difficulty lies in the fact that drought is a relative term; it all depends on what is taken as the standard. In some areas, droughts follow a regular pattern; they hit southern Africa roughly once every 18 years and the Great Plains of North America every 20 years, for example. But in many parts of the world they are notoriously unpredictable. In fact, a drought is defined as a continued absence of *expected* rainfall. In Britain we claim to be in the throes of drought if there is a period of at least 15 consecutive days with no more than 0.2 mm of rain: in the world's drylands a period of several months, or even years, without rain may be considered quite normal.

As far as the immediate problems in Africa are concerned, the controversy over climatic change is partly academic. The question to ask is: While severe droughts have occurred in the Sahel many times in the past, why haven't they had such a devastating effect as they are having today? And the answer is simple. Drought itself may be an act of God, but the Sahelian famines are not. What is happening is that certain countries, and certain people, are becoming more susceptible to the inevitable food shortages which occur when droughts strike.

Politicians prefer to ignore this and are often tempted to place the blame for their starving people on the lack of rain alone. It allows them to throw their hands up in horror – and, once the excitement has died down, to do nothing about it. As they rightly say, many countries that suffered famines during the 1980s also experienced severe droughts – and no one can control the climate. But they choose to forget that we could control the political, social, economic and ecological issues which conspire with drought to increase the suffering.

What makes people susceptible to famine?

Famine-stricken countries in the Sahel generally have several things in common, apart from drought.

- They have experienced major population explosions, which mean that there is not enough food to go around.
- Their people are so poor that they do not have the money to buy food in times of need.
- They spent long periods during the 1980s in a state of civil war.
- Their traditional agricultural practices have either been abandoned or do not produce sufficient food.

In 1950 the population of the Sahel was 47 million. It is forecast to reach 159 million by the turn of the century, and 263 million by the year 2020. The population of Ethiopia has been increasing by just under 3 per cent annually; this means an extra 1.3 million mouths to feed every year. Food production has increased healthily in the Sahel (contrary to the popular misconception) and, ironically, 1988 saw bumper harvests throughout the region. But these have not been able to keep pace with such a rapid population growth, so the amount of food produced per person has actually declined. The situation is similar in many parts of the world – there are too many people for the farmers to feed.

But this is only a small part of the story. A large proportion of food production in the developing world is for the 'wrong' reasons. For those countries without mineral or oil wealth, cash crops are a major source of foreign exchange, so the farmers have been growing these in preference to food crops. Cotton and peanuts, for example, sell for much higher prices abroad than sorghum and millet can fetch in the local markets. During the 1980s melons were being exported from Ethiopia to earn badly-needed foreign exchange while millions of Ethiopians were starving. But there was enough food in the country for those who could afford to pay. In the words of one researcher, 'A general shortage of food is hardly ever the cause of famine. It is the poverty of victims, who are unable to purchase the food that is available.' Even with food aid, corruption at all levels often results in the food donations being sold to those who can pay, leaving the poorest people to starve. A famine would not occur in Britain or North America, because extra food would be imported – at whatever price – and there are various safety nets to prevent large numbers of people starving to death.

The worst aspect of poverty is that it is a trap – self-sustaining and self-generating. It is forcing millions of people, and many governments, to destroy the very resources on which they depend. People are forced by hunger to eat the grain they had planned to sow the following season, thus continuing the famine for at least another year. Governments are forced to pursue ecologically reckless policies to keep up with their foreign debt repayments.

War disrupts societies and economies. People are forced to flee their land to avoid the fighting; more than 600,000 Mozambicans have fled over the border to Malawi from the ferocious civil war between the Marxist government and Renamo rebels. With military disturbances, even when food aid is received, the supplies do not always reach the people in need. In fact, controlling the supply of emergency food aid is often used to political advantage; the inflexibility of the Sudanese government in getting food supplies to the war-torn south of the country during the 1980s forced many aid agencies to pull out of the Sudan – they felt that they were being manipulated politically.

The fourth common link is an ecological one. One of the key factors affecting the incidence of famine is a process called desertification, an ugly term which literally means the making of a desert. It is the final link in a chain of events causing habitat degradation. Unlike many other habitats, deserts are not under threat; indeed, many people believe that they are actually increasing in size. They can be formed naturally, through climatic changes, but in recent years a range of human activities are thought to be causing them to expand at an alarming rate.

The term desertification was first coined in the 1940s by a French forester working in West Africa. He used it to describe a gradual degradation of the environment there, as he witnessed trees being cut down and human pressures on the land leading to a slow spread of desert-like conditions. But desertification did not become international news until it was associated with the African famines of the early 1970s. Then scientists began to realise that it was happening not only in the drylands of Africa, but throughout the world.

THE ENCROACHING DESERTS

The final stage of desertification is the loss of soil fertility, or the loss of soil altogether through wind and water erosion. Soil can take centuries to form, but is a delicate substance and can be destroyed very easily. It may not be much to look at – a curious assembly of mineral particles, air, water, organic matter and tiny animals – but without it, and the plants it supports, we could not survive.

The expansion of the world's deserts is therefore as worrying as the shrinking of other habitats. According to some experts, every year desertification claims an area of land nearly twice the size of Belgium, damaged beyond repair. The United Nations Environment Programme has estimated that 30 per cent of the earth's land surface is threatened in this way.

Deserts can spread as a result of climatic change, but most desertification is caused by human mismanagement of the land. So it is vital to know why this is happening.

What is a desert?

Sand dunes, camels and heat are perhaps the most familiar images of a desert. Endless seas of drifting sand are certainly typical of many desert areas but some, such as the Gobi Desert of eastern Asia, have very few sand dunes. Similarly, camels are animals that have adapted well to the rigours of the desert environment, but many deserts do not have camels at all. It would even be wrong to say that deserts are always hot. The Gobi is actually quite cold in the winter, and at night the temperature in many deserts drops to below freezing; when the sun goes down, there is no cloud or tree cover to keep the day's heat near the ground, so it escapes quickly and easily.

But as desertification proceeds apace, and desert gains a foothold, there are two features that become increasingly apparent. The vegetation gradually disappears, leaving bare expanses of stony or sandy ground; and there is a severe lack of water.

Most deserts receive very little in the way of precipitation – the word used for all forms of atmospheric moisture, including rain, fog, dew, hail, snow and mist. London receives 620 mm in an average year, while the desert city of Timbuktu receives just 220 mm. But lack of water does not mean simply a lack of rainfall: it is sometimes available from other sources. For example, the Namib Desert, north of the Kalahari in south-west Africa, is unusual in that it borders a coastline; at night, fog sometimes rolls in from the sea and, as it drifts over the desert, condenses into droplets. Water availability also depends upon other factors, such as temperature. For example, London's average annual temperature is 11 °C, whereas in Timbuktu it is 29°C. The little rain that Timbuktu does receive is rapidly evaporated.

The nature of desert rainfall is also important. It is notoriously sporadic. In some places it rains once every few months, in others only once every few years. When the rain does finally arrive, it comes in fierce torrents that fade almost as soon as they begin. An area typically receives an intense downpour equal to its entire annual average – although, in this sense, the average does not mean quite the same as it does in Europe; we expect certain months to be wetter than others but, compared with the rainfall in a desert, ours is quite evenly distributed throughout the year. Desert rainstorms are also different because they can be very localised. Whereas in Britain we receive most of our rain from depressions which sweep in from the Atlantic and soak most of the country, desert rainstorms occur in relatively small areas. A few square kilometres may receive a torrential downpour, while all around remains perfectly dry.

The changing desert boundary
Life itself is at the limits of endurance in the desert environment. Even plants and animals living along the desert margins have to be well-adapted to the unpredictability of its fragile land and harsh climate. They have developed ways of resisting water loss, or retaining moisture; some are opportunistic feeders or simply migrate away when conditions get too bad; others remain in suspended animation for many months, or even years. But when it rains, the landscape can change overnight from an apparently dead wasteland to one awash with colour and activity. The desert literally blooms as seeds suddenly germinate, plants rapidly grow and flower and animals leap into life in the newly greened landscape.

It is this dynamic nature of desert margins which makes it so difficult to distinguish between areas which are simply lying dormant and those which have been damaged and will not leap into life when the rains eventually return. The fact that the Sahel has been suffering a more or less continuous drought since the end of the 1960s may have coloured the views of some scientists who are too eager to identify desertification in areas which are simply responding in their normal way to drought conditions.

This is not to belittle the scale of the desertification problem. There may be doubts about it, but there is not enough time to wait until we are 100 per cent certain of all the details. Instead, it is a word of caution; making the distinction between drought and desertification is crucial because the appropriate action necessary to relieve any suffering will be different in each case.

What causes desertification?

Human activities are believed to cause desertification in several ways – through overcultivation, overgrazing, vegetation clearance and even unsuitable irrigation schemes. During severe droughts the damage being done becomes very obvious, because the desert is given a chance to leap forward. But desertification is such a slow gradual process that usually we hardly notice it happening.

People frequently overwork soils to the point where they can no longer produce food or fodder. It happened in Greece two millenia ago; it has happened elsewhere many times since. In the 1930s American farmers worked their land so intensively that vast areas were turned into a dust bowl. We are still making the same mistake today, on every continent in the world.

A piece of agricultural land can withstand a certain amount of cultivation, or can support a certain number of cattle, sheep or goats, without suffering any loss of quality. But if it is never given a chance to recover its supply of nutrients and organic matter, the soil becomes exhausted; or, if too many animals are grazed on the land, all the vegetation is eaten and their hooves cause erosion. The productivity of the land, and the health of the animals, gradually declines. Devoid of all vegetation, the soil is then exposed to the ravages of wind and water erosion, which leave desert in their wake.

The situation in Africa is particularly bad, although at one time the lifestyles of Sahelian farmers were perfectly adapted to suit their fragile and unpredictable homes. The herders roamed the land with their animals in search of the plants that spring up when it rains; and they knew when to move on in order to preserve the pasture for subsequent return visits. The cultivators were more settled, growing drought-resistant millet and sorghum which were ideal for the local conditions; they used a farming system called shifting cultivation, where some fields were allowed fallow periods (to give the land time to recover) while others were being cultivated. The two groups would trade their products – cereals for milk and meat – to enrich their diets. And if times were particularly hard, everyone relied on wild plants and bushmeat, which naturally persisted even during severe drought.

But all that changed with the colonial era, which distorted the economies of the traditional farming systems, and of Sahelian countries, to supply Europe with raw materials. The early colonists stopped the herders moving their animals across European-owned land. They forcibly took the best land from the cultivators, replaced fallow periods with artificial fertilisers and swapped their traditional crops with alien cash crops, such as cotton and peanuts, for export back to the western countries. The peasants were forced to move north into the desert fringes, confined to smaller and smaller areas. They had to abandon their traditional lifestyles and watched helplessly as the grasslands deteriorated.

Today national policies often follow the old colonial ones and more people are being pushed into the marginal lands along the southern fringes of the Sahara. Political boundaries have become barriers to the herders' free migrations, and government policies force them to settle where they can be controlled and taxed. Farming for local consumption very much takes second place. Increasingly large areas of land are used to grow cash crops, and modern livestock rearing projects have been introduced, to earn foreign exchange for importing technology. These are themselves leading to large-scale desertification problems and, to make matters worse, the money earned is being spent on military defence or huge development projects, such as dams and roads, which bring few rewards to the peasants.

Dryland vegetation is chopped down by the local people for two main reasons: to prepare the land for cultivation; and to collect wood for fuel. The effects are similar to those of overcultivation and overgrazing, with the loss of vegetation exposing the soils to erosion. Further problems arise when most of the fuelwood near a settlement is cleared. The little wood available is then supplemented with dried animal dung, which would otherwise be left on the land to act as a natural fertiliser.

Irrigation of dryland soils should be able to solve many of the food production problems by ironing out the vagaries of sporadic unreliable rainfall, but many irrigation schemes are badly designed, with little or no drainage. In areas which are poorly drained, the groundwater level below the soil surface begins to rise as the land is irrigated. As it does so, evaporation by the hot desert sun increases the concentration of its salts. When the salty groundwater reaches the plant roots, it retards their growth. Ultimately it causes a decline in crop yields. Irrigated dryland soils sometimes become completely waterlogged and have a white, salty crust on top. No plant life can survive under these conditions and the land has to be abandoned.

The mythical advancing wave
Reports on desertification tend to use a litany of statistics to support their arguments. So many have been quoted so many times that they are now accepted without question. But the truth is that we do not yet have all the facts and figures.

In particular, we are told that deserts are advancing in inexorable waves, engulfing all productive agricultural land in their paths. It is a forceful and emotional image, but a very misleading one. Desertification rarely progresses in this wave-like manner: much more common is a pattern of gradual degradation in patches of land well away from the desert edge. These expand and coalesce to give the impression of gradual advance. Thus desertification has been likened to *dhobi* itch – a ticklish problem in delicate places.

It is an important distinction to make, because one frequently quoted solution to the desertification problem is to plant a belt of trees to halt this advancing tide. It has even been suggested that trees should be planted right across the Sahara's southern fringes. Thick vegetation in a dry landscape is a very visible sign that something definite is being done, but a green belt of this kind does not tackle the real problem.

FIGHTING FAMINE

In 1977 hundreds of international experts met in Nairobi, at the headquarters of the United Nations Environment Programme, to devise a plan of action to combat desertification. Since then millions of pounds have been spent, by the UN, aid agencies, governments and non-governmental organisations, to implement the plan and counter the problem. But considering its urgency, and the huge sums of money invested, surprisingly little has been achieved.

In terms of population, the Sahelian governments receive more foreign aid – in the form of money, emergency relief and technical assistance – than any other part of the world. But aid is not simply a matter of channelling money from the haves to the have-nots, and many people are cynical about its real value. It has certainly had varied results. Some aid has been tremendously beneficial, some completely ineffective and some utterly disastrous, even aggravating the situation.

Foreign aid is often given on the understanding that, in return, goods and services are bought from the donor country – 'We will give you aid, if you buy our tractors.' For example, 80 per cent of Canadian aid is tied in this way. And the choice of aid projects is often influenced by the donor's own commercial, political and military aspirations; a great deal of money goes into the farming of cash crops, for example, to enable the recipients to export food and raw materials wanted by the donor countries. The bulk of assistance from the United States goes to strategically important countries, a third of it (even in the Sahel) in the form of military aid.

Another problem is corruption. The critics complain that aid is all about giving to rich people in poor countries. This is at least partly true; corruption ensures that up to 30 per cent of the aid never reaches poor people, but is siphoned off into private bank accounts and slush funds. Or it is spent on 'cathedrals in the sand' – grandiose projects, such as dams and roads, which impoverish the poor still further and enrich the élite.

Despite its ambiguities, emergency relief, as opposed to foreign-government-funded aid, has rather clearer and more simple goals. But the fact that it too has problems illustrates the difficulties involved in a longer term approach. Non-governmental organisations such as Band Aid and Oxfam manage to get a much higher proportion of their aid to the poor than most government agencies. This is partly because governments have to channel aid directly through other governments, which then sell it; this in turn can undermine the prices of the little food available in local markets, thus destroying the livelihoods of local farmers. It has even weaned farmers away from growing their own crops altogether, totally destroying local food production and causing the recipient countries to become increasingly dependent on food aid. Ultimately, it can be addictive and destroys the traditional ways of coping with emergencies.

The problem is accentuated by the fact that the aid often arrives too late, long after the droughts have ended. It took the EEC more than a year longer than promised to get food to Ethiopia during the 1984–5 drought, because of so much red tape and bureaucracy. It is also true that a great deal of food aid is not quite as it sounds; it has as much to do with disposing of agricultural surpluses as with helping the poor.

With all these problems, the situation in the Sahel has worsened, not receded as some had predicted. But because the Sahelian countries rely on foreign aid so much, aid agencies have a relatively high degree of power to promote policy changes in the region. Many approaches have been tried, and many have failed. But desertification can be arrested and reversed. While we do not yet have a complete picture of the processes involved, enough is known to take decisive action; and there is a great deal to learn from past mistakes.

Environmental solutions
An urgent requirement is the development of early warning systems, which identify the underlying problems in time to take evasive action before drought strikes. In the Sahel, drought itself cannot be predicted or controlled, but it can be planned for.

Experience in Africa has shown that grain is usually delivered between four and six months after an emergency request, simply because of the logistics involved. Once it arrives at its initial destination, there are further delays because of shortages of planes, trucks or trains, so it accumulates in overloaded docks and airports. Then no one has any idea where it is most needed.

Following the famines of 1984–5, a new system for combating future disasters was established by the United States government. It was called the Famine Early Warning System, or FEWS, and was set up precisely to identify the people and regions most at risk from famine before the crisis hits. FEWS currently has field operations in Mauritania, Mali, Burkina Faso, Niger, Chad and Sudan, and operates with supplementary back-up information from satellite imagery and other research in the States. The basic principles for this valuable effort are enlightening. It makes three important assumptions:
- Famine is a slow process that takes two or three years to develop.
- Famine and drought are not necessarily related.
- The direct causes of famine are political, social and economic.

The long-term solution to famine must take account of all these causes – it must be prevention rather than cure. Dealing with the underlying ecological problems requires fieldwork, which has been seriously lacking in the past. Conferences and documents on famine, drought and desertification have multiplied almost to the point of becoming a minor industry, while relatively few resources are channelled into field projects.

The aim should be to help the peasants of the Sahel to help themselves, by relieving some of the stress under which they have to operate. Compared with them, we actually know very little about how their environment works. Traditional farming techniques are often portrayed as backward, inefficient and unproductive. But they are not. After all, they have not broken down in the past. They are perfectly adapted to producing food, under difficult conditions, for individual families and communities. But they only work without pressure and regulation from outside. Past experience has already shown that we cannot impose our own measures without reference to local knowledge, and expect them to be successful. Workable solutions will therefore combine traditional techniques with new ideas.

It is also important to develop a network of protected areas across the Sahel. There are currently 180 parks and reserves in the region, covering nearly 200,000 square miles, or 5 per cent of the total area. These seemingly non-productive areas are more than a luxury. They preserve the region's genetic resources, such as plants tolerant to drought and heat; they provide opportunities for research, to learn about how the ecosystem functions; they offer scope for tourism, which could be an alternative source of foreign exchange; they stabilise water run-off from watershed systems; and they protect soils. They may even contribute to the stability of the Sahelian climate by maintaining natural vegetation cover.

Solutions to the more sensitive issues

Environmental solutions to famine in the Sahel will be short-lived unless something can be done about the many other problems facing traditional societies and governments in the region.

Almost all the people affected by famine in the Sahel are subsistence peasants – people with no money and little political clout. Their needs are usually ignored. It is important to find ways of restoring power to their communities to give them more freedom to manage their own land, as they did in the pre-colonial era.

But poverty is the greatest problem. We must find ways of making the poor people of the Sahel more prosperous, which requires the development of national economies throughout the region. This is precisely how the richer countries of the world have succeeded in preventing famine themselves. We could help to make a start by importing more from the Sahelian countries, and paying higher prices for it, while selling our own manufactured goods to them for less. We should also help to reduce the burden of their foreign debts; since 1982 the developing world has received less money in aid from the entire industrial world than it has paid out in interest on its foreign debts.

Several conservation groups (including WWF) have been developing a possible solution to this problem. They have reached debt-for-nature deals with various governments in the developing world, under which specific conservation work and land protection is guaranteed in exchange for paying off a proportion of the national debt. This was first tried in Bolivia in 1987, after a substantial discount had been negotiated with the donor, and was very successful. Other participants since have included Costa Rica, Ecuador and the Philippines. WWF's first debt-for-nature swaps in Africa took place in August 1989 and involved a US$3 million swap with Madagascar and a US$2.27 million swap with Zambia.

The system is not without its critics. And these figures are, of course, just a drop in the ocean of international debt. Hundreds of millions of dollars would need to be released to make a significant long-term impact, which would require debt-swapping at government level. But it has great potential for the Sahel, dealing as it does with the two burning issues of the region – sustainable land management and the burden of mounting debts.

In Ethiopia, WWF is working in the still largely unspoiled Bale mountain range in the south of the country. Many of the country's rivers rise here, and flow south into the fertile areas where agricultural productivity can be maintained. By helping the Ethiopians to protect this vital watershed area, WWF hopes to prevent further erosion of habitat and loss of species.

Niger in sub-Saharan Africa is increasingly arid. The few remaining trees were being cut down for firewood or to build houses. The WWF project team based in Niger brought Arab craftsmen down to demonstrate how adobe houses using mudbricks could be built – and the WWF headquarters was one of the first buildings to be constructed in this way. Slow-burning, economical cooking stoves were imported to reduce the amount of wood needed for fires.

5 THREATENED SPECIES

Ninety-five per cent of all animals and plants that have ever lived on earth have become extinct. Pterodactyls, sabre-toothed tigers, mammoths, woolly rhinos, giant ground sloths and many millions of others have disappeared in the past. No species is guaranteed a life of more than a few million years before it evolves into a new form or forms, or dies out completely. This process of extinction is a normal and healthy aspect of nature that has been happening since life originated on earth some four billion years ago. Why, then, is there so much fuss about species threatened with extinction today?

The answer is simple: the extinction rate is soaring as a direct result of human greed and stupidity. Hunting, pollution and the international pet trade are not just vague threats – they are wiping out one species after another. Most important of all, habitats are being lost at an alarming rate and, without them, there can be no animals or plants. Yet we continue to burn and fell tropical rain-forests, turn rich soil into desert, drain important wetlands, dam rivers, build roads through ancient woodlands and detonate coral reefs.

For millennia one animal or plant became extinct roughly once every 100 years. But nowadays the extinction rate is believed to be nearer 1,000 species every year. And by the end of the century the world may be losing one animal or plant every hour. Many people think of the extinction of the dinosaurs as sudden and catastrophic and, indeed, in terms of the overall age of the planet it was. But it probably took longer for them to disappear than the entire time that people have been on this planet, which puts the current extinction rate into perspective.

It was the dodo that first gave us the concept of man-made extinc-tions. The largest and strangest member of the dove family, it was found on the island of Mauritius in the Indian Ocean. Dodos were very trusting birds and, since they were unable to fly, made easy prey for the sailors who visited their island home during the 16th and 17th centuries. So many were clubbed to death for food and sport that, by about 1680, the last one had been killed and the species had gone forever.

The dodo is famous for being extinct. But we know very little about which species we are plunging to extinction today. Many animals and plants are disappearing even before we know of their existence, perhaps hidden away somewhere in a quiet corner of a tropical rainforest or in the depths of an unexplored sea. Although perhaps this should not be surprising when you consider that we know more about the surface of the moon than we do about parts of our own planet.

Only a small proportion of all the species in the world have been discovered, identified and described. Centuries of study by thou-sands of biologists have so far revealed 1,030,000 animals and 370,000 plants, but some experts believe there could be as many as 30 million species altogether. It is as if we have read only the first five pages of a 100-page book.

New species are being found all the time. Many of these are small, obscure and, to some people, perhaps rather dull. But there have been some undeniably exciting finds in recent years. The golden bamboo lemur was found in Madagascar in 1986; a giant gecko was discovered in Iran in 1987; in 1988 a new muntjac deer was found in China and a tree kangaroo in Australia; and another Malagasy lemur, the golden-crowned sifaka, was identified in 1989. But by the time many of these new animals (and plants) have been discovered they are already threatened with extinction and they could disappear altogether before the experts learn enough about their requirements, and the threats to their survival, to save them.

If current trends continue, one species in 15 could be extinct by the middle of the next century. A glance at the many volumes of *Red Data Books* (the authoritative sources of information on the world's threatened species) gives some idea of the scale of the problem. Published by WWF's scientific partner, The World Conservation Union (formerly known as the International Union for Conservation of Nature and Natural Resources, IUCN), the books name 4,589 animals which are known to be in danger of extinction – 555 mammals, 1,073 birds, 186 reptiles, 54 amphibians, 596 fishes and 2,125 invertebrates. Many of these are familiar species, including the mountain gorilla, giant panda, humpback whale and California condor; but the majority are less well-known (but equally important) ones such as the sucker-footed bat, milky stork, San Francisco garter snake, golden toad and the big South Fork crayfish.

Plants have their own *Red Data Book*, but it would take many volumes to cover the estimated 60,000 species that are seriously threatened with extinction. Many of these are also likely to disappear by the middle of the next century. And this would be the greatest loss of plant species that has ever occurred in such a short period of time.

Some of the creatures on these danger lists are so rare that there are now few survivors left. However even the smallest populations can be brought back from the brink, although it is a desperate race against time when there are only, for example, 43 kakapos, 25 northern white rhinos, 20 Hawaiian crows, 14 echo parakeets – and just one surviving *Hyophorbe amaricaulis* palm tree.

But for others there is no guaranteed safety in numbers. The likelihood of a species becoming extinct depends upon the nature of the threats it is facing, so that even apparently safe ones are sometimes at risk. For example, the North American passenger pigeon was once the commonest bird that has ever lived on earth; huge densely-packed flocks, which darkened the sky and could take three days to pass overhead, were a common sight in the middle of the 19th century. But pigeon hunting became a full-time occupation for thousands of men; the birds provided the cheapest meat available at the time and demand for them was phenomenal. Pigeon hunting also became a popular sport, a single hunter easily killing 500 or more birds in a single day. The result was that the last passenger pigeon to be seen in the wild was shot by a young boy on 24 March 1900; and on 1 September 1914 the last member of all the species, affectionately called Martha, died in captivity in Cincinnati Zoo. The hunters had accomplished the impossible, in less than 50 years.

The fate of the passenger pigeon is perhaps the most unbelievable and astonishing of all extinctions. But history is repeating itself. Twice a year in the Mediterranean millions of migratory songbirds are persecuted indiscriminately with guns, traps, nets and limesticks. In Africa elephant and black rhino populations are being decimated by ruthless gangs of poachers, after their tusks and horns. In the Pacific Ocean hundreds of thousands of dolphins are killed every year by tuna fishing operations. And there are many more examples from all over the world.

The passenger pigeon and the dodo served as warnings which, tragically, we have so far ignored.

WHAT ARE THE MAIN THREATS?

Cynics might argue that animals and plants fall basically into four categories.
- The first includes all those species which are obviously beneficial to people; they are hunted and poached, or collected for research and the international pet trade.
- The second consists of all those which are regarded as pests, or feared in some way; they are killed on sight, trapped or poisoned with toxic chemicals.
- The third includes the animals which are supposedly fun to kill and, consequently, are shot by sports hunters.
- The final category consists of all the innocent bystanders – the species that have no obvious benefit or sports value, though, at the same time, are not considered to be a nuisance. But even these suffer indirectly from many other human activities; pollution, the introduction of exotic species, competition with domestic animals, international trade, disturbance at breeding areas and, most important of all, the continuing destruction of natural habitats, threaten the survival of all the world's wildlife.

Habitat destruction
Habitat destruction is the single most important danger to wildlife. We are destroying the natural places where animals and plants live at a rate even more frightening than the speed at which we are capable of hunting individual species to the point of extinction. In addition, habitat loss is far worse because it is harmful not only to a single kind of animal or plant but to entire ecological communities. It affects

common and threatened species alike.

Tropical rainforests, in particular, are disappearing at an alarming rate – currently by an area five times the size of Switzerland every year – and these forests are home to half of the species in the world. Some unique regions have disappeared already; when a single ridgetop in Peru was cleared recently, more than 90 different plants known only from that locality were lost forever.

But no habitat is safe. There are few parts of the world which have not been altered, damaged or destroyed. Even the North American tundra has been invaded by the trans-Alaskan oil pipeline, while some of the world's most isolated islands are disappearing under hotels and aircraft runways. Many countries have virtually no unspoilt habitats left, or just small remnants surviving amid great expanses of farmland and sprawling cities. And now these remnants themselves are beginning to disappear; in Britain, hundreds of rare snakes and lizards are dying as the remaining fragments of Dorset's once extensive heathland is being built upon.

Even protected areas are at risk. Coto Donana National Park in southern Spain is one of the world's most valuable wetland reserves; it is on a major migration route for birds flying between Europe and Africa, and is an important refuge for lynx, otters, flamingos, imperial eagles and many other species. Yet it is seriously threatened by the excessive use of ground water (for the irrigation of surrounding farmland) and by plans to build a beach resort; water is being pumped from the area faster than it can be replenished, and at least one lagoon has dried up. In Uganda, Murchison Falls National Park is now threatened by a 480-megawatt hydroelectric power project which would seriously reduce the water flow in the Park, affecting fish and other wildlife. A similar project was proposed in the 1960s, but abandoned in 1971 after fierce opposition from environmentalists. Yet now Uganda's energy minister argues that water levels in Murchison Falls are already so low that it is no longer one of the world's natural wonders.

Modern technology is partly to blame because it speeds up the process of habitat destruction. Nowadays serious damage can be done in a fraction of the time that it would have taken years ago. It is possible to fell an entire forest in a day, or to build a large housing estate in a matter of months. Modern technology is also having a profound effect on the scale of the damage being done. A single dam can quickly replace a huge fast-flowing river with a permanent deep valley lake, while a six-lane highway can be cut through mountains and deserts, meadows and forests with relative ease.

Much of the damage that has already been done is irreversible; animals and plants, unlike people, cannot simply adapt overnight to a new kind of habitat, or disperse to find alternative, unoccupied places to live. Yet as the human population grows, even greater pressure is being placed upon the few natural areas that are left.

Many species are so seriously threatened by habitat destruction (their ranges are reduced and their numbers diminished to dangerously low levels) that they are poorly equipped to deal with any further threats they may have to face.

Hunting and poaching

Hunting is the most obvious cause of extinction. The earliest known members of the human lineage – Australopithecines and, more recently, hominids such as Neanderthal man – lived largely by hunting. Prehistoric man was also a hunter, killing wild animals with spears fashioned out of wood and stone. For the most part their impact upon wildlife populations was minimal but, as early peoples spread across the globe, they plunged a number of species to extinction. When people arrived in Australia, for example, some 25,000 years ago, one in three of the larger marsupials there disappeared.

But the effect of hunting on wildlife in recent years has been considerably more devastating. The late 19th and 20th centuries have seen a wave of extinctions and population declines perhaps unprecedented in the history of the world. One of the reasons is that with modern firearms and extensive transport facilities, the only restraints on the number of animals being killed are self-imposed by the hunters.

Few examples illustrate the destructive powers of hunting better than the American bison, or buffalo as it is often known. Three hundred years ago as many as 60 million bison wandered over the prairies and open forests of North America; single herds of hundreds of thousands of the animals were commonplace. The local Indian tribes had depended on the bison for many years, eating the meat and using the hides to make clothes, tepees and canoes. But with their simple hunting methods they killed relatively small numbers and had no effect on the bison population.

However, when the European settlers arrived on the continent and, particularly, when they began to sweep westward in the 1860s, a mass slaughter began. The white men killed enormous numbers of bison – specifically to deprive the Indians of their wild herds, but also to free the land for farming, to obtain the animals' tongues and hides, and for sport. The bison were slaughtered without difficulty by hunters on foot, on horseback and, later, even from the comfort of passenger trains. About 2.5 million were killed annually from 1870 to 1875 and the legendary 'Buffalo Bill' Cody claimed to have killed 4,862 buffaloes in one year alone. By the late-1890s the bison was virtually extinct in the wild.

Fortunately, a few hundred had been kept in captivity and the species has managed to survive, thanks to an extensive captive-breeding programme. There are now more than 50,000 of them, living mostly in protected areas.

On the other side of the world, in Asia, tiger hunting became a popular sport at the time when the bison was already on the verge of extinction. Earlier attempts to hunt tigers, with spears or bows and arrows, left the odds in the animal's favour and made no impression on their numbers. But with the advent of modern weapons (which could kill a tiger from several hundred yards away) and with the unfortunate enthusiasm of British army officers and senior civil servants, tiger hunting became a very popular sport. So many were killed that several Indian maharajahs, who organised hunts as great social occasions, claimed to have shot more than 1,000 of the animals each.

Sixty years ago there were still 100,000 tigers living in a variety of different habitats in Asia, and they were so common in some areas that one Indian naturalist commented that 'it was a question whether man or the tiger would survive'. But by 1970 the hunters had killed so many that there were only four to five thousand left. Two races of tiger – the Caspian and Balinese – had already become extinct, and the Chinese and Javan tigers had been reduced to just a handful of survivors. But a major conservation effort called Operation Tiger was launched two years later and, by giving the animals legal protection and providing them with special reserves, the species was saved from extinction. Nowadays there may be as many as 7,500 tigers in the wild, although their future is still uncertain. Relatively few live in protected areas, and even those are seriously threatened by habitat disturbance.

The llama-like vicuna which lives in the high central Andes of South America was also hunted to the brink of extinction. Vicuna produce, reputedly, the finest wool in the world. The Incas used to shear them to make fabrics for their royalty and prized the animals so highly that anyone caught killing one, without direct authority from the state, was sentenced to death. But the Spanish colonists decided that herding and shearing vicuna was much harder work than removing the wool from dead animals, so that by the mid-1960s hunters had killed more than a million of them and just small herds were left, hidden in a few remote and inhospitable areas. Conservation became an urgent priority. In the late 1960s and 1970s special reserves were set up and the governments of Bolivia, Chile, Peru and Ecuador agreed to strict protective measures. There are now estimated to be more than 85,000 in the wild.

Nowadays, there is at least some kind of legal protection for many threatened species, but it can be very hard to enforce, especially when there are strong political or financial incentives to break the law. For example, it is illegal to kill black rhinos and, in most countries, African elephants, but poachers continue to hunt them for their horns and ivory; western lowland gorillas are protected in Gabon, but sometimes appear on the menus of restaurants in the country's main towns; there is currently an international whaling moratorium, but great whales are still being hunted by several different nations; and even giant pandas are sometimes killed illegally for their skins.

It is also very difficult to protect animals that are caught by accident during other hunting activities, such as deep-sea fishing; 500,000 Brunnich's guillemots die in fishing nets each year off the west coast of Greenland, for example. Gill-nets are especially dangerous, because they are designed to entangle fish or squid instead of capturing them inside special pouches; but every year salmon gill-nets in the North Pacific kill nearly one million seabirds, 20,000 Dall's porpoises, 700 fur seals and many other animals.

The world's fisheries are approaching a catch size that is near the maximum sustainable harvest – the annual catch that can be taken year after year without depleting the natural breeding stock. This is reckoned to be 100 million tonnes. The figure is calculated only for conventional fish – those species for which a large market currently exists. The 1986 catch was around 84 million tonnes which, at current rates of increase, will reach the maximum sustainable harvest by 1991.

As if to bear this hypothesis out, already a number of major world fisheries have collapsed or are showing signs of overfishing. In the Mediterranean Sea, the Black Sea and the north-west Pacific catches have already exceeded their regional maximum sustainable yields.

The FAO lists a number of species which have been most severely overfished in recent decades, most of those occurring in temperate waters. They include the king crab, Pacific halibut and Pacific ocean perch in the northern Pacific; the South African pilchard in the South Atlantic and the capelin, Atlantic cod, Atlantic herring and haddock in the North Atlantic. In the North Sea, dwindling stocks of herring and cod have necessitated strict cutbacks on the fishing quotas set by the European Community for 1989 catches. The total allowable catch (TAC) for North Sea haddock was cut by 60 per cent, from 164,000 tonnes in 1988 to 62,500 in 1989; for cod the TAC reduction was not as great – 20 per cent, from the 1988 quota of 150,000 tonnes to 118,700 tonnes in 1989. But fishery scientists are convinced that the declining stocks are the result of overfishing and overcapacity, as more efficient fishing methods have masked the dwindling numbers.

One alarming result of this overfishing occurred in the North Atlantic in the 1970s; heavy fishing of herring and mackerel from the north-east Atlantic continental shelf off North America is believed to have caused what marine biologists term a biomass flip. This occurs when a previously dominant species in an ecosystem declines and the population of another species rises rapidly. In this region, herring prey on sand eels and sand eels prey on herring larvae; mackerel prey on the larvae of both species. The result of overfishing the herring and mackerel was that the predatory pressure on sand eels was relaxed and their numbers exploded.

Wildlife trade

International trade in wildlife is worth about US$5 billion a year and involves thousands of different species. It is centuries old, although there has been a dramatic increase in its volume since the 1950s. In recent years, public awareness, stringent conservation measures and dwindling wildlife resources have gradually reduced the level of demand in some countries, but it is still sufficiently high to be putting many species seriously at risk. Much of this trade is legal and openly advertised, but a significant part of it takes place on the black market – as long as there are people who want certain wildlife species badly enough, there will be others who are willing to supply them.

There are two parts to the trade:
- Live animals and plants, which usually travel by air.
- And animal products, which often travel by sea.

Most consignments come from developing countries and are supplied to buyers in the United States, western Europe, Japan and other parts of the industrialised world. The trade involves some very large commercial enterprises and well-organised crime syndicates. There are huge profits to be made and improved transport systems enable traders to ship consignments anywhere in the world. The illegal operations use channels and methods not unlike those used by international drug smugglers.

Most of the wildlife products are in demand for luxury goods such as perfumes, aphrodisiacs, jewellery or fur coats; others are used in pharmaceuticals or for investment purposes. For example, snake skins are used for making belts and wallets; the musk from Himalayan musk deer to make perfume; the skins of spotted cats to make coats; butterflies and moths for mounting in glass cases; frog's legs are imported for sale in restaurants; and any animal unfortunate enough to possess large teeth is vulnerable to attack from the trinket trade.

Fortunately attitudes are changing gradually in some parts of the world. At one time in Zaire there was considerable demand for gorilla skulls and hands, which poachers sold as tasteless souvenirs; but most of the tourists and expatriates who bought them out of ignorance as recently as ten years ago would not dream of doing so now.

However there is still great demand in many countries for rare and exotic pets, posing a major threat to some of the smaller monkeys, colourful birds, reptiles, tropical fish, butterflies, spiders and many other creatures. And some very ingenious, and ostensibly legal, methods have been devised to meet this demand. For example, the smugglers use forged or altered documents; they combine a few captive-bred animals (which sometimes can be traded without restriction) with wild-caught ones in the same consignment; they pack a few rarities with a large number of similar, but much commoner, species, on the assumption that they will not be noticed; or they simply label the animals or plants incorrectly, in the hope that the customs officials will not be very good at wildlife identification. There have even been cases where birds with easily-recognisable, brightly-coloured plumages have been temporarily dyed black.

Alternatively, the animals are smuggled from one country to another hidden amongst other cargo or in a variety of unlikely places. Hummingbirds are stuffed into cigar tubes, rare snakes have been threaded into coat lining, and monkeys are squashed into the false bottoms of crates. The animals are given virtually no room to move – for journeys that may last several days. Sometimes they are deliberately packed to be completely immobile, thus avoiding give-away scuffling noises as they pass through customs. Indeed, conditions are often so appalling that the trade is routinely based on the principle that many of the animals will die; officially, 196,454 birds were imported into Britain in 1989, but the total number of casualties was probably many times that figure. Animals that leave an exporting country alive represent only a fraction of the ones that were caught;

enormous numbers are killed or maimed during capture, or die before they can be shipped. Even larger numbers succumb to their long journeys, due to stress, injury, overcrowding, poor hygiene, hunger, thirst, cold temperatures or infection.

For example, over 200,000 parrots are imported into the EEC member states every year, with up to four times as many dying in the process of capture and transportation. When tens of thousands of tortoises were being imported into Britain, 80 per cent of them died while being shipped or during the first year in their new homes. Similar numbers of tropical fish are also dead within a year of purchase.

Live animals are also traded for the testing of new chemical products and for biomedical research. There is strong evidence of wild-caught chimps arriving (illegally) in laboratories in Japan, western Europe and the United States. Chimps are considered essential scientific 'guinea-pigs' because they are susceptible to virtually every illness that afflict humans. The one disease they do not appear to suffer from is AIDS, which in itself has accelerated the demand for new animals. Some scientists are now willing to pay as much as US$25,000 per chimp.

Chimpanzees are also being smuggled into Spain for use as photographers' props, nearly 200 of them being dressed in children's clothes and forced to pose with tourists. Now 200 may not seem a large figure, but behind the scenes lies a distressing story that is typical of the international wildlife trade. The animals are worked for up to 16 hours at a time, on the beaches during the day and then in the bars and nightclubs until the early hours of the morning. Once they are about two years old they are heavily drugged to keep them manageable and docile; then, after another couple of years, when they have grown too big and have begun to frighten the tourists rather than attract their sympathy, they are either drowned or abandoned by their owners. In the wild, a healthy chimpanzee can live for up to 40 years.

All the chimps that have been smuggled into Spain come from the forests and savannas of West Africa. They are difficult and dangerous animals to catch. When a family group is found, the adults have to be shot before the local hunters can grab all the youngsters. Bullets are often too expensive, so they use flintlocks, loaded with stones or metal fragments, to fire at the chimp families. The newly-captured babies are then transported to Spain, perhaps squashed into the false bottom of a crate or even, as in at least one case, disguised as a human baby. Often they are dead on arrival. For every animal that does manage to survive, ten others probably have died *en route*. This means that the lives of 2,000 chimps may have been lost to obtain the 200 working in Spain today. Since there are only 50,000–200,000 chimpanzees left in the wild, the trade is a serious threat, particularly when considered in combination with local hunting for meat, poaching for biomedical research and habitat loss.

The Spanish chimp problem has received a great deal of publicity in recent years, but the international trade in wild plants is relatively little known. Millions of plants are dug up, packaged and sold every year to meet the growing demand for garden plants and houseplants in North America, western Europe, Japan and elsewhere in the world. Since virtually all of them are collected from the wild, the effect has been devastating. Turkey is one of the worst offenders, but many other countries are losing their wild flora to the trade – the more exotic the plants, the greater the demand, and the rarer they are, the higher the prices they fetch. Cactuses, orchids and insectivorous species are especially popular. Many of them can be artificially propagated, but it is often cheaper for traders to buy wild plants than cultivated ones.

Cactuses in particular can survive out of the soil for a long time, making them relatively easy to transport, so the level of trade is astonishing. For example, 50,000 rainbow cactuses are removed from Texas every month; and so many golden barrel cactuses have been dug up that the species is thought to be extinct in the wild, although, ironically, it is still a common plant in collections. One quarter of the cactus family is now in danger of extinction.

Rare orchids are among the most valuable of all plants, a single specimen selling for as much as US$5,000 to a keen collector. But as always the people who make the big money out of the trade are not the peasants, hunters or poachers but the middlemen and the wealthy dealers. Even the common orchids are popular because, very often, they are equally attractive. One catalogue published recently in the United States listed 700 orchid species from three different continents. But they are usually traded as bulbs and, since even botanists cannot easily identify them without their flowers, it is often impossible to tell the difference between common and threatened species.

Human carelessness and disturbance

Animals and plants are harmed accidentally in the course of many human activities – plants are trodden on, seals and manatees are wounded by the propellers of motorboats, snakes are run over by lawnmowers and ducks get tangled up in discarded fishing line.

In many parts of the world, particularly in coastal areas, people and wildlife compete for space. But just a human presence can be very disturbing for animals such as terns, turtles and seals when they are at their breeding colonies.

There is a current example on the Greek island of Zakynthos, in the Ionian Sea. Zakynthos has the largest known rookery of rare loggerhead turtles in the Mediterranean, with roughly 2,000 occupied nests on the island each season, but it is also a popular holiday destination, attracting more than 30,000 tourists every year, and the common interest in Zakynthos is not a happy one.

The turtle nesting season is from mid-June to mid-August which, unfortunately, coincides exactly with the main tourist season. The turtles sensibly wait until the safety of darkness before coming ashore to lay their eggs at the back of three favoured beaches. Each female digs a large hole, kicking the sand away with her back flippers, in which she lays about 100 round, white eggs roughly the size of table tennis balls. She then carefully covers them before making her laborious trek back to the sea. The young hatchlings, no more than a couple of inches long, will emerge seven or eight weeks later. Most fall prey to a variety of different predators, including rats and herring gulls; only a lucky few will survive long enough to breed themselves.

As recently as the early 1970s tourists were virtually unknown on Zakynthos. The turtles and the 30,000 local inhabitants had always coexisted without conflict. But now the island has an international airport, with more than 70 chartered flights arriving every week. It is possible to hire mopeds and cars, there are many large hotels and the latest hit records blare out of beachside tavernas. And many tourists (80 per cent of whom are British) have said that they chose Zakynthos in preference to other holiday destinations specifically because of the turtles, which are used by several tour operators to promote the island. But even the most conservation-minded people can cause problems in large numbers. Scores of sunbathers unwittingly stamp and tread on the turtles' buried eggs during the day, crushing them or making it impossible for the hatchlings to get out. And at night, everyone wants to go turtle-watching, armed with torches and cameras that, not surprisingly, frighten the animals into abandoning their nesting attempts.

When the hatchlings first emerge from their nests they are attracted to the sea by its bright surf, and repelled by dark patterns at the back of the beach; it is a good natural system, making sure they crawl in the right direction. But street lights and tavernas attract them instead and increase the risk of predation while they struggle to reorientate themselves.

These conflicts of interest are difficult to solve. A great deal of pressure has been put on the Greek government to restrict access to the most important nesting beaches and to protect the turtles in other ways, but there is considerable opposition from local people because, although they wish the turtles no harm, tourism is the main-stay of their island economy. A ministerial decision came into force in 1982 (and was improved in 1987) which controls or prohibits building work in the most important nesting areas; another decision, to expropriate all land in some of those areas, was particularly unpopular.

Legislation of this kind is important, but difficult to implement. There are now barriers across the main access points, to keep cars away, and guards to keep people off the beaches at night. These are certainly steps in the right direction, although it is too soon to tell whether they are working. Providing information to the tourists is equally important; there are already two information centres, free leaflets, evening slide shows in some of the hotels and morning walks to demonstrate how the nests are being monitored.

In the long term, if the nesting beaches can be protected ade-quately, it might be possible to arrange carefully organised night-time vigils to watch the turtles. These would have to be for small groups, and under strict supervision, but could ultimately benefit everyone on Zakynthos – the turtles, the tourists and the local resi-dents.

The introduction of alien species

For centuries people have taken animals and plants with them on their travels around the world. Early colonisers were often accom-panied by stowaways, such as rats and mice, and they had a nasty habit of taking their favourite birds and mammals with them, to release for sport or for sentimental reasons. Even today, animals are imported to control unwanted pests, and many other foreign species are kept in captivity and then allowed to escape.

The result is that a motley collection of rats, mice, cats, dogs, goats, mongooses, snakes, fish, ants, privet and other wildlife have found their way to virtually every corner of the globe. Whether they are introduced deliberately or accidentally, they cause a variety of problems:

- Bringing parasites and diseases.
- Disturbing ecosystems.

- Feeding on native animals and plants.
- Competing with them for food, shelter and space.

In Britain there are a number of introduced species, including some rather unlikely ones such as red-necked wallabies and ring-necked parakeets. One of the most familiar is the North American grey squirrel, which was introduced during the 1800s simply out of curiosity, to see if it would survive. It not only survived but positively thrived, and today occurs in suitable habitats throughout much of the country. However it has made itself unpopular by becoming a serious woodland pest and a notable predator of eggs and young birds.

Britain has also suffered from its fair share of invading disease organisms, which can be particularly dangerous – in some parts of the world they have wiped out entire populations very quickly. For example, Dutch elm disease, which probably arrived in Britain in logs imported from Canada, reached epidemic proportions in the country in the 1970s. Millions of trees died, threatening several other species as well, such as the white-letter hairstreak butterfly whose larvae feed on elm.

Island ecosystems have always been susceptible to biological invasions. Their native plants and animals are rarely adapted to cope with either predators or competitors, and have nowhere to escape to if the going gets tough. Island species the world over have suffered the consequences.

The small Indian mongoose was introduced to Jamaica in the late 1800s in an attempt to control rats which were damaging the island's sugar cane plantations. The mongooses were very effective and ate most of the rats, as intended. But they then turned their attentions to other animals. As a consequence, some of Jamaica's native reptiles, birds and mammals have become extinct and many others are gravely endangered.

On the other side of the world, two different snakes (the Philippine rat snake and the Australian brown tree snake) have been introduced to Guam since the 1950s and are now eating the eggs of native birds, with some serious results.

Round Island, off the north coast of Mauritius, is regarded by many conservationists to be one of the most important islands for its size anywhere in the world. Little more than a square kilometre in area, it probably has the highest concentration of threatened species. In particular, it is home to four reptiles that are found nowhere else in the world (the keel-scaled boa, burrowing boa, Telfair's skink and Guenther's gecko) and the only known wild population (eight individuals) of the bottle palm. Round Island is also important because the wildlife that survives there was once found on pristine Mauritius, where much of it became extinct after privet, guava, rats, monkeys, pigs, deer and other alien species arrived. Luckily, rats never made it to Round Island, but rabbits and goats were released there during the last century, and their excessive grazing destroyed the hardwood forest and much of the other vegetation. This resulted in widespread erosion, so that most of the soil was washed into the sea, turning the land into a moonscape, with just small vestiges of native vegetation left. It was miraculous that any of the island's wildlife managed to survive at all.

During the 1970s there was a major effort to eradicate the two culprits. The last goat was shot in 1979, but the rabbits were more evasive and were not removed completely until 1986. Within a year the island was beginning to show signs of recovery, with grasses and young trees appearing in areas that were formerly bare. Returning Round Island to its original condition is considered by many to be one of the most important conservation efforts of recent years.

Another well-documented example is Stephen Island in New Zealand. Two square kilometres in area, it lies in Cook Strait, between South Island and North Island. It was once home to a unique bird called, appropriately, the Stephen Island wren. The first time anyone saw the wren was in 1894, when the lighthouse-keeper's cat caught one and took it home to eat. Unfortunately, the cat caught another 15 in rapid succession – and they turned out to be the last of the species. The Stephen Island wren became extinct in the same year that it was discovered. At roughly the same time cats were introduced to Mangere Island, a long way off the east coast of New Zealand's South Island, to control rabbits. But they also developed a penchant for birds and ate every representative of 12 species, three of which were found nowhere else in the world and so became extinct.

Islands are subject to more biological invasions than ever before as the expansion of shipping, fast plane services and international trade have made it easier for all kinds of plant and animal species to be carried far outside their original ranges. And people continue to introduce animals and plants intentionally, despite the known risks involved. On the Pacific Island of Moorea, in French Polynesia, seven different land snails recently have fallen victim to a species introduced from abroad. Their fate was sealed by an attempt to control the giant African snail, which had been introduced to Moorea in the 19th Century by the European governors who wanted a good supply of juicy specimens for snail soup. Some of the animals managed to escape and spread across the island, becoming pests by eating crops. In 1977 another snail was introduced to prey on the giant African snail, but it decided to eat the native species instead. Within ten years, although six survived in captivity, all seven native snails were extinct in the wild.

Introduced plants can also do serious harm. Two aquatic species, water hyacinth and a kind of water fern, have brought widespread changes to lakes and marshes throughout the tropics. Water hyacinth is actually toxic to fish and the fern has caused some dramatic changes to the ecology of Kenya's Lake Naivasha.

Pollution

Pollution occurs in many forms – as a solid, liquid, gas or energy, as heat or noise. It can occur as a result of natural processes, such as when volcanic eruptions release gases and ash into the atmosphere; and it is a byproduct of many different human activities. The variety and impact of human-related pollution has increased dramatically in recent years, and is such that it seriously threatens human health, destroys habitats and kills animals and plants in most parts of the world. Every year thousands of millions of tonnes of deadly substances, from factories, power stations, ships, vehicles, houses, agriculture and other sources, are released into the environment. Some of the substances are unnatural; others are natural but are released in large quantities, or in unnatural forms (such as the industrial discharge of hot water).

Pollution is everywhere – in the air, on the land, underground, in freshwater, in oceans and even in the tissues of plants and animals. Sometimes it kills animals and plants outright; at other times its effects are subtle, but no less harmful. Some of the worst problems are caused by landfills, pesticides, oil and sewage.

More than 90 per cent of the world's domestic and hazardous wastes are disposed of in landfills, which are often just holes in the ground. In many cases these holes allow toxic chemicals to pollute groundwater, despite the official theory that biological and chemical processes will render dangerous substances harmless. Even containment sites, lined with impermeable materials such as clay or plastic, can overflow after heavy rain, and no lining can be leakproof forever.

The use of chemical pesticides is increasing at the rate of more than 12 per cent each year. World production in 1986 was about 2.3 million tonnes; in the United States 1.8 kilogrammes of pesticides are used every year for every American. And pesticides can harm wildlife, people and the environment in a number of different ways. They kill other animals and plants as well as (or even instead of) the target species. They contaminate the food and crops on which they are sprayed – most food nowadays contains pesticide residues. And they seep into freshwater supplies, killing fish and contaminating ground-water. A survey in 1985 on pesticides currently being used in Britain suggested that 49 were possible carcinogens, 61 may cause birth defects and 90 are possible allergens. Many more toxic pesticides are used in the developing world, where there are few restrictions on their use; they are imported from industrialised countries, where they are banned or severely restricted.

One of the most useful and effective of all pesticides is DDT. It remains active in the environment for many years and therefore saves farmers the trouble of repeated spraying. But once it has been ingested, DDT is stored in the fatty tissues of animals and is concen-trated as it works its way along the food chain. By the time it reaches predators such as birds of prey it is being stored at concentrations hundreds of thousands of times greater than that at which it was first applied. One of the effects in birds is to interfere with the chemistry of eggshell formation – DDT makes the shells so thin that they break when the adult birds sit on them. Its use has caused serious population declines in peregrine falcons, ospreys, bald eagles and many other species. DDT is now banned in most industrial-ised countries, but exports to the developing world continue unabated.

There have also been a number of accidents at factories making pesticides, releasing vast quantities of the chemicals into the envi-ronment. In 1986 a fire broke out at the Sandoz chemical factory near Basel in Switzerland, releasing more than 30 tonnes of pesticides, fungicides and chemical dyes into the River Rhine. The river was rendered lifeless along a stretch of more than 100 miles.

Oil spills have increased steadily since the loss of the *Torrey Canyon* off the south-west coast of England in 1967, despite serious international efforts to control them. Every year more than 3.5 million tonnes of oil are released into the world's oceans, representing 1 tonne for every 1,000 tonnes excavated from beneath the earth. Oil slicks are particularly lethal to seabirds and some mammals, and destroy marine and coastal ecosystems.

In the 1970s oil was in fact the most serious marine pollutant – from wrecked tankers, from tanks washed at sea, from seabed wells and from oil terminals. But the oil problem has been greatly contained since the mid-1970s, according to a recent major review of the health of the world's oceans; for example, accidental oil spills have decreased, although specific events such as disasters in Antarctica and Alaska in 1989 still cause very severe ecological damage in certain areas.

On 24 March 1989 the *Exxon Valdez*, a 30,000-tonne oil tanker, disembowelled herself on a series of underwater reef pinnacles in Prince William Sound, Alaska. She was outside normal shipping lanes, with the captain absent from the bridge, and was loaded with 240 million litres of crude oil.

The impact ripped open eight cargo tanks and 50 million litres of oil spewed into the sea. The oil was quickly broken up by the vagaries of the wind and the local currents, and eventually was washed up in three national parks, four national wildlife refuges and on to nearly 2,000 kilometres of near-pristine shoreline.

Eleven thousand men and women struggled for weeks to save the local wildlife and begin the long task of clearing up the mess. Despite their efforts, though, the final death toll was appalling: a US federal government agency estimated that the spill had claimed the lives of more than 300,000 seabirds and millions of fish; many other dead animals were found, including 950 sea otters, 150 bald eagles and nine whales – perhaps just a fraction of the total of wildlife that had succumbed to the spill.

The *Exxon Valdez* was the worst tanker disaster in US history. The clean-up operation alone has cost the Exxon Corporation more than a billion dollars, and more than 150 lawsuits have been filed against the company for negligence.

Despite such catastrophes, though, sewage and the dumping of industrial waste are now the main marine pollutant problems. In many countries human sewage is channelled through systems of underground pipes to special treatment plants. However, in some coastal areas raw sewage is pumped straight into the sea untreated, while in much of the developing world there are few treatment facilities inland. India has 3,119 towns and cities, of which only eight have the facilities to treat their sewage fully, while 209 are able to carry out only partial treatment; this leaves a total of 2,902 towns and cities in the country with no sewage treatment at all.

Sewage effluents contain large quantities of nitrates and phosphates, which cause eutrophication. This is a process by which lakes and rivers become over-fertilised; the chemicals act as nutrients, stimulating the growth of algae and, when the algae die, the micro-organisms that decompose their remains use up all the oxygen from the water during the decomposition process, so that the lakes and rivers eventually become foul-smelling and virtually lifeless. Nitrate fertilisers also cause eutrophication in some areas, such as East Anglia in

Britain, by draining into waterways from surrounding farmland.

Natural organic pollutants like sewage are eventually decomposed and, once the source of pollution has been removed, it is possible for ecosystems to recover. But if the damage has been particularly severe, or the pollutants are more permanent, the ecosystem suffers the consequences for a long time. In the last 100 years pollution has irreversibly changed many habitats all over the world.

The most sewage-polluted seas are those off the densely populated shores of south Asia – off Pakistan, India, Bangladesh, Sri Lanka and the Maldives. A rapidly-increasing 950 million people live along these shores, with a quarter of them making their living from the polluted seas and their contaminated products. But coastal cities the world over are all too often temped to pump domestic wastes into a seemingly all-absorbing sea, this temptation outweighing the cost of adequate sewage treatment plants.

Industrial wastes are also poured straight into the sea, both from coastal plants and, via rivers, from inland sites. There are few parts of the world where industrial pollution is not yet a problem. Oxygen levels in many coastal waters, such as around Karachi in Pakistan, in the northern Adriatic and around many built-up areas of the Arabian Gulf, have been so depleted by chemical pollution that their life-supporting capacity is seriously impaired.

The Baltic Sea is the largest area of brackish water in the world. It receives freshwater from some 250 river systems, giving the sea a rather low salinity compared to the open ocean. It has a surface area of 366,000 square kilometres (just 0.1 per cent of the surface area of the world's oceans) and is bordered by seven countries – Sweden, Finland, the Soviet Union, Poland, East Germany, West Germany and Denmark. Since the early 1960s the Baltic has been severely affected by pollution. Its drainage area contains at least 200 major industrial complexes, mostly steel and metal works, chemical industries and pulp and paper mills. Pollutants from these industries, combined with excess nutrients from agricultural run-off (annual loads of 1.1 million tonnes of nitrogen and 77,000 tonnes of phosphorus have been calculated) have combined to leave an estimated 100,000 square kilometres of the sea virtually dead – so starved of oxygen that almost no marine life can survive. In the summer of 1988 the pollution problem was so bad that, for the first time, most of the beaches of the Baltic were closed.

Toxic substances including mercury, DDT and PCBs have accumulated in Baltic marine plants and animals. While levels of mercury in fish have been reduced in some coastal areas during the 1980s, and a ban on DDT in the Baltic states has cut DDT levels in fish substantially, levels of PCBs have not fallen. And it is PCBs that have been blamed for reducing the reproductive rate of female grey seals from 80 per cent to 20 per cent.

Progress in reducing the quantities of toxic pollutants reaching the Baltic has been largely the result of a decade of effort by the Baltic Marine Environment Protection Commission (otherwise known as the Helsinki Commission, or HELCOM) which was set up in the 1970s as a joint venture by all the Baltic states. Although HELCOM has no power to enforce its decisions, they are expected to be incorporated into national legislation. At their meeting in March 1988 the states agreed to cut by 50 per cent their inputs of nutrients, heavy metals and organic toxins by 1995. On a wider front, with the help of similar agreements HELCOM is becoming a model for international environmental cooperation.

The Caribbean Sea has also been hard hit by pollution. Like other regional seas, it is semi-enclosed and therefore has slow rates of water renewal, making its cleansing capacity lower than that of the open oceans. Pesticide run-off and industrial effluents are the main threats to the ecosystem. Large quantities of pesticides reach the sea from the United States via the Mississippi, which drains 41 per cent of the continent. Many other pesticides, banned in the United States, find their way into the sea from the 16 Latin American states bordering the Caribbean. Industrial pollutants, particularly from sugar refineries, mining, offshore oil-drilling and the pumping of dredgings and industrial waste, have had severe effects on the sea's fragile ecology. The Gulf of Paria, between Trinidad and Venezuela, has been particularly badly hit by discharges of industrial waste.

The East Asian seas form an area of intense economic activity through trade, shipping, oil production, offshore mining and commercial fishing. In many parts, fishing grounds have been polluted, coral reefs mined and mangrove swamps destroyed. Oil pollution, from shipping and offshore rigs, is a major source of pollution in this area, but sewage and other municipal wastes from major conurbations such as Bangkok, Kuala Lumpur, Manila and Jakarta are another destructive source; Singapore is the exception, treating 80 per cent of its sewage. Furthermore, sedimentation from agriculture, logging, mining and construction is also a major source of marine pollution in the region. The resulting turbidity of coastal waters reduces primary productivity by blocking out sunlight, added to which many sediments contain concentrations of toxic heavy metals.

HOW DO YOU CONSERVE WILDLIFE?

Many wildlife extinctions of the past were caused by ignorance. But we no longer have that excuse. We have a much more detailed understanding of the environment and of the policies that are needed to save threatened species from extinction. There are still many gaps in our knowledge, of course, and research will always play a critical role in wildlife conservation. But in most cases we know enough to take action. The main stumbling blocks are political and economic.

The approach to wildlife conservation has changed a great deal in recent years. It is becoming more realistic. The fact that the struggle for day-to-day survival will always take precedence over wildlife is now widely accepted and means that there is no way of protecting animals and plants unless the basic needs of people are satisfied. So the only way of addressing this problem is to combine conservation with development. This is why so many far-sighted wildlife projects are now based on the principle that the interests of wildlife have to be commensurate with the needs of people.

Habitat protection

Habitat protection is essential for three reasons:

- The destruction of habitats is the most important threat to wildlife.
- It is pointless protecting individual species unless they have somewhere safe to live.
- It takes into account the fact that no species lives in isolation – they are all part of a complex web and rely on one another.

The bottom line is that, without suitable habitats, there can be no wildlife.

It also has the hidden advantage of protecting many species all at once, including ones we do not even know exist. In tropical rainforests, for example, large reserves protect countless numbers of animals and plants, some of which are known but many of which are not. One 50-hectare plot of lowland forest in Malaysia has been studied intensively and found to contain no fewer than 835 species of trees; true, this is a world record, but it illustrates the advantage of protecting areas rather than species.

Many parks and reserves have been set aside for wildlife; the number of sites more than doubled between 1975 and 1990. Some countries are even combining their efforts in order to protect common areas of importance. It is particularly encouraging that a joint wilderness reserve is being planned between the United States and the Soviet Union, for land on both sides of the Bering Strait, where Siberia and Alaska are just 50 miles apart.

But there is no cause for complacency. Protected areas still cover only a tiny fraction of the most important ecosystems in the world, and, simply because an area is protected on paper, it does not mean that it is safe. It is not enough merely to establish a protected area and hope for the best. It is essential to manage the land in order to improve or maintain prime conditions for wildlife. This may include the removal of undesirable animals and vegetation (especially introduced species) and controlled burning or grazing to maintain important plant communities. There may also be a need for regular patrols to prevent poaching or trespassing. And if public access is allowed, roads and footpaths have to be constructed and maintained, as well as information centres and other facilities.

International pressure is sometimes needed to persuade countries to establish a sufficient number of suitable protected areas. The so-called Ramsar Convention was one of the first attempts to do this by imposing external obligations on the land-use decisions of independent countries. The convention, otherwise known as the Convention on Wetlands of International Importance especially as Waterfowl Habitat, is designed to protect wetlands of international importance. It came into force in 1975 and in 1990 had some 52 signatory countries and more than 460 listed wetlands. Each contracting country's main obligation is to designate at least one wetland of international importance for inclusion in a formal list. Contracting countries also agree to promote the conservation of the wetlands they have designated and to aim at the wise use of all their wetlands. Unfortunately, most parties have been reluctant to designate sites that were not already protected before they joined Ramsar – and some of the world's most important wetlands are not protected, partly because they are in countries that have not yet signed the convention.

Existing national parks and reserves tend to be relatively small and fragmented. There are many with boundaries which cut across migration routes of the very species they are trying to protect and others which have small isolated populations with no access to fellow members of the same species. It is as if protected areas have become islands, surrounded by farmland and human habitation, and cut off from the rest of the world.

This is a particular problem facing giant pandas in China. Pandas were once widespread throughout the country but now occur only within a restricted range in the mountains of south-west China, there being between 400 and 1,000 survivors in total. Pandas feed on bamboo, many varieties of which follow 50- or 100-year cycles; at the end of each cycle, the plants bloom, drop their seeds and die. In ancient times, when bamboo died in one area, the pandas were able to move elsewhere, but nowadays they survive only in little pockets of bamboo forest surrounded by farmland and, when the plants die, they have nowhere else to go. As a result, more than 150 pandas have starved to death in recent years.

The key to the success of many protected areas is the involvement of local communities. There are few countries in the world that can afford to conserve wildlife just for the sake of it. The old belief that wildlife should not be tampered with is unrealistic and impractical in these days of so much human hardship and poverty. Wildlife has to work for its living – and be seen to be doing so.

In Zambia, perhaps more than in many other countries, the wildlife is particularly rich and could be put to good use in improving the lives of many hundreds of thousands of people. This does not, however, mean that indiscriminate slaughter is the way to go about it. Wildlife resources should be regarded as biological capital. Using them sustainably is the same as spending the interest – without eating into the capital itself. In Luangwa Valley, a range of activities are being developed – such as hippo cropping, game meat co-operatives and safari hunting – with considerable success.

In India, an early oversight of Project Tiger was the lack of any effort to do this. Consequently, despite its enormous success in saving the tiger from extinction, it now faces a new challenge from India's expanding human population; basically, it is impossible to keep people out of tiger reserves. Most of these reserves (there are 18 altogether) are surrounded by people, who need firewood for cooking, fodder for their livestock and forest plants for their food and traditional medicines. And if the natural resources outside protected areas are depleted, the local inhabitants have no choice but to go inside the reserves; some 50,000 domestic animals depend on Ranthambhore National Park for fodder, for example.

But Project Tiger is now developing a new system of village ecology, which is simply the integration of land and people. An excellent example is the Palamau Tiger Reserve in Bihar, which successfully combines wildlife conservation with the sustainable use of natural resources. The reserve has a fully protected core area, for wildlife, and a large buffer zone for local villagers. The people graze their cattle and harvest forest products such as bamboo, grass, wood and wild fruit, and are employed in the construction of patrol roads, guard huts and firebreaks. As a result, their own future is more secure, and they have a vested interest in the future of the reserve.

The concept of marine parks and reserves is relatively new; marine conservation efforts in the past have been largely restricted to solving pollution problems and to protecting individual species such as whales and dolphins. But despite all the difficulties involved, an increasing number of countries are establishing marine reserves with considerable success.

Australia's Great Barrier Reef Marine Park is the world's largest marine protected area. It stretches some 2,000 kilometres along the continental shelf off the north-east coast of Australia, encompassing 2,600 separate reefs, shoals and coral formations in an area of 350,000 square kilometres. It was established in 1975 after public outcry over proposals for oil drilling and mineral exploitation on the reef. And in 1981 it was put on the World Heritage List.

The living reef, one of the most diverse ecosystems on earth, is made up of 400 different coral types. It is home to 1,500 species of fish, 4,000 species of molluscs and 240 bird species which nest on the islands. It also supports one of the main feeding grounds for the endangered dugong, nesting grounds for six species of turtle, and is frequented by whales, dolphins and many other creatures.

The Great Barrier Reef Marine Park Authority has the power to regulate and prohibit activities within the park. The park's management plan divides the area according to six zones. These range from general use, where all activities except mining are allowed (although some require permits), to highly restricted scientific and preservation zones, where permits are required for all of a restricted number of activities; in scientific zones, for example, these activities are traditional fishing, traditional hunting and scientific research, while in preservation zones only research is allowed.

The park's objective is to promote human enjoyment and use of the area, consistent with conservation of the ecosystem. But with more than 100,000 tourists visiting the reef every year, uncontrolled tourism and speculative developments continue to threaten some areas above the low water mark – areas which are not adequately protected by the Great Barrier Reef Marine Park Act of 1975. Fears have also been raised about invasion of the reef by the crown-of-thorns starfish, whose digestive juices break the coral down while they are feeding. A survey showed that more than one-third of the reef had been invaded by the early 1970s, and experts fear the whole reef could die within 50 years – but the huge concentrations of starfish disappeared in late 1973. There may have been smaller outbreaks since but the cause is still a subject of controversy. But it may be a natural occurrence and it seems that the reef is recovering slowly.

Legislation

Since it is usually impossible to rely simply on goodwill for conservation action, it is important to have specific obligations to protect wildlife. Legislation therefore plays a critically important role in wildlife conservation.

International treaties are necessary because many species live in more than one country – or they live in the sea, which is predominantly no-man's land. Furthermore, the entire international community is involved in one way or another with wildlife trade. So it is important for a treaty to gain the support of as many countries as possible. Every country is free to decide whether or not it wants to join. The Bonn Convention, which is devoted specifically to protecting migratory animals, is a good example of the way conventions are weakened by lack of support. It provides that: migrants must be protected in all the countries they visit or pass through. Formally known as the Convention on the Conservation of Migratory Species of Wild Animals, the Bonn Convention came into force in 1983 and is potentially a very powerful conservation tool. It is unusually wide-ranging and has particularly strict requirements, but this in itself has discouraged many countries from joining and, as a result, it only has about 30 parties. The whole treaty is considerably weakened without complete coverage of the most important migration routes.

Just flicking a legislative pen, however, is not enough. Unfortunately many bureaucrats seem to think they have done the job simply by signing an agreement or putting a law on the statute book. But the standard of protection afforded by a treaty is always as weak as its weakest link and, to have any effect, it requires effective law enforcement. This in turn requires real commitment by the countries concerned, dedicated staff – and money.

The strongest and most widely supported of all international wildlife laws is CITES – the Convention on International Trade in Endangered Species of Wild Fauna and Flora. It began with just ten parties in 1975 and has since expanded at an astonishing rate. At the time of writing, it now has an impressive total of 106. But there are still loopholes in the treaty, and it is still widely abused by some member states and many wildlife smugglers.

Protection under CITES is provided in two main categories. The most endangered species are listed in Appendix I to the Convention; these are the ones that are threatened with extinction and are, or may be, affected by trade. No permits for trade in these species are issued, except under very special circumstances. Among those listed in this category are all the apes, giant panda, great whales, tiger, both elephants and all rhinoceroses, many birds of prey and some mussels, orchids and cacti. Appendix II to the Convention lists other species at serious risk which might become endangered if trade in them is not controlled and monitored. International trade in these is permitted with proper documentation issued by the government of the exporting country. The species in this category include all the primates, cats, otters, whales, dolphins and porpoises, birds of prey, crocodiles and orchids that are not covered by Appendix I, as well as many others such as fur seals, birdwing butterflies and black corals.

CITES is ultimately the responsibility of member states; in practice, it is customs officers who enforce it in most countries. But wildlife smuggling continues on a large scale, for many reasons:

- The national legislation to implement the Convention is inadequate.
- Penalties for illegal trading are too low.
- There are few well-trained customs officials.
- There is a lack of adequate facilities for holding live animals.
- Some of the documents and licences are easy to forge.
- In most countries, an extremely low priority is given to controlling wildlife trade.

Another interesting international treaty is the Polar Bear Agreement, which was signed in 1973 by all five circumpolar states – Canada, the United States, the Soviet Union, Denmark (for Greenland) and Norway. The polar bear population dropped sharply during the first half of this century (when sport and commercial hunting was rife) and could only be protected by a truly international agreement; polar bears love to travel and move freely around the Arctic with no respect for political boundaries.

The Agreement has three main objectives:

- To restrict the killing and capturing of polar bears.
- To encourage and coordinate research.
- To protect the polar bears' ecosystem.

It has proved very successful, despite the lack of a permanent administrative structure or regular meetings. Polar bear hunting has been banned in the Soviet Union since 1955, and in Svalbard since 1973, but elsewhere in the Arctic the treaty allows for some bears to be killed by traditional hunters. Roughly 600 are taken in Canada (including up to 15 by licensed sports hunters using Eskimo guides), 100 in Alaska and 150 in Greenland. This is out of a total polar bear population of around 25,000.

One of the main problems of any international treaty is that there is no way (other than public and diplomatic pressure) to force contracting parties to comply with the regulations. This does not apply to national legislation, which can be enforced directly by the police and the regular judiciary system.

In most of the developing world there is little protection for wildlife outside official national parks and reserves; and even where suitable laws do exist, enforcement is extremely lax or non-existent. It is often difficult, or prohibitively expensive, to patrol the more isolated parts of some countries and there is a general lack of knowledge about the laws themselves. Many industrialised countries do have reasonably satisfactory wildlife laws, but a similar lack of knowledge – and often a lack of interest – hinder their implementation.

Captive breeding

Captive breeding is usually viewed as a last-ditch attempt to save a species from extinction, or as an insurance policy, in case other conservation efforts go wrong. But keeping threatened animals and plants in captivity does provide the opportunity to glean information about them which could prove vital when future conservation programmes are developed. And an incidental benefit of captive breeding is that it makes threatened species visible to the general public; with the help of imaginative educational programmes they can make a valuable contributin to public awareness of their plight.

Threatened species have been bred in captivity for nearly a century. Even the earliest efforts, to save the American bison and, at around the same time, China's Pére David's deer, were successful in bringing critically small populations back from the brink of extinction. But captive breeding is by no means straightforward. When a species becomes very scarce, it suffers from inbreeding – all members of the population are closely related and harmful genetic characteristics tend to accumulate. One of the main problems is infertility, which occurs when there is a lack of genetic variability.

But considerable expertise in juggling captive populations has been developed in recent years. Botanic gardens keep extensive seed banks, in case there is a need for rejuvenation in the future, and there are some high-tech methods of freezing animals' eggs and sperm for the same reason. Another important technique is the use of international studbooks, which were started for some species as early as the 1950s. These enable zoos and captive breeding centres around the world to keep a track of the degree of inbreeding when they bring new animals into their collections.

Some species have become extinct in the wild and survive only in captivity. One of these is an extraordinary bird, the California condor. With a wingspan of 2.7 metres, it is one of the largest flying birds in the world. It was once widespread throughout many parts of the south-western United States, but was persecuted and poisoned (through bait left out for coyotes) for many years, and pesticide poisoning caused a thinning of their eggshells. By the early 1940s there were between 60 and 100 left, and the population was continuing to decline steadily.

The decision to take them into captivity was a difficult one, as it always is under such circumstances. But the decision was made and by 1988 all known California condors were in either San Diego Wild Animal Park or Los Angeles Zoo. There were 28 birds altogether. The following year four eggs were laid and all the chicks survived. The total population now stands at 32, 18 of which have been raised from eggs.

Also in the United States there are plans to reintroduce rare black-footed ferrets to their former home in the north-western state of Wyoming some time in 1991. At the turn of the century black-footed ferrets were fairly common throughout the Great Plains of North America, but their numbers declined as the Plains were turned into farmland and their prairie dog prey was subjected to an enormous poisoning campaign by farmers and ranchers. At one point the ferrets were feared extinct, but a new colony was discovered in Wyoming in 1981. By 1985, when the population had dropped to fewer than 130, it was decided to bring some into captivity. Three males and three females were captured but, to everyone's horror, they died within a few days. They had canine distemper, which the experts suddenly realised was at large in the last-known wild colony. The following weeks and months were spent catching as many of the ferrets as possible, with the result that there were a total of 17 in captivity by February 1987 – and they were all safely vaccinated. In the meantime the wild population had become extinct.

The black-footed ferrets are now well on the road to recovery (at a cost of more than US$2.5 million, so far) and the total population is up to 124. They will be reintroduced to the wild when there are more than 500 of them, the aim being to establish at least ten separate groups, with more than 30 ferrets in each – although some will always be kept in captivity just in case anything goes wrong.

If reintroduction is impossible it is obviously better to have some survivors in captivity than to let the species become extinct. But the long-term aim of any programme of this kind is, one day, to return the captive-bred animals or plants to their natural homes. This has been achieved with considerable success on a number of occasions, a classic example being the beautiful and distinctive Arabian oryx, which became extinct in the wild in 1972. Although once common throughout Arabia, it was wiped out in less than 30 years by hunters with fast cars and automatic rifles. Fortunately, in anticipation, a small number of the animals had been taken to zoos in Arabia and the United States ten years earlier. They have bred successfully and, now that hunting is no longer allowed, are gradually being reintroduced to their desert homes in Oman, Jordan and most recently, Saudi Arabia. It is a particularly enlightened project because it enlists the help of local nomadic people; in Oman, the Harasis tribe is employed (very successfully) to guard the animals as they wander over the desert.

The Arabian oryx was the first example of returning captive-bred animals to their original habitat after the extermination of the entire wild population, but there have been a number of others since. One of these is the Mauritius kestrel which, in 1974, shot to fame as the rarest bird in the world – there were just six left. It was decided to capture two of them and, after a series of trials and tribulations, the species bred successfully and dozens have since been returned to their natural homes. There are now nearly 100 in the wild, including 12 breeding pairs.

The more habitats are destroyed, the more important captive breeding will become. But in some cases, when animals and plants can be protected round-the-clock in the wild, there is no immediate need to bring them into captivity; instead they can be kept under semi-wild conditions. A number of important orchid sites are actually fenced off, to keep people and grazing animals out, even though such sites still require constant attention and vigilance: fences tend to attract people's attention, causing even more disturbance than usual; and artificial grazing is often necessary, to reduce the competition for light and space from other plants. In some ways, a secret location without a fence would be safer than a well-known one with a fence; this is why a few orchid sites are never revealed publicly.

Another last-ditch solution is to move animals and plants from threatened habitats to safer ones. This is known as translocation, and has been pioneered by the New Zealand Department of Conservation in recent years. Threatened birds of several species, including saddlebacks and kakapos, have been translocated from the mainland to offshore islands which are free of rats and other introduced predators, with considerable success.

Captive-bred or semi-wild animals and plants can also be used, in some circumstances, to meet the international demand for wildlife in order to reduce the strain on wild populations. This is, perhaps inevitably, a controversial approach. Apart from anything else, it is an unpleasant way of achieving conservation aims. Another major criticism is that, once the animals and plants are on the market, it is often impossible to tell whether they have been bred in captivity (or artificially propagated) or collected illegally from the wild. However, it may be the only solution in some cases. Dwindling wild plant populations, for example, cannot cope with the demands of the international trade indefinitely, so it makes sense to encourage the traders to breed their own plants rather than relying on wild stocks. The traders benefit in the long term because they rely on a steady supply; and the buyers benefit because cultivated plants are healthier and usually live for longer. But the plants themselves will benefit only if it results in a declining demand for wild stocks. This may be achieved by establishing cultivation centres in the countries of origin, which can provide secure, safe and reliable incomes for the plant collectors.

It was a decline in wild crocodile and alligator populations in the early 1960s that first led far-sighted conservationists and traders to investigate the possibility of farming the animals on a sustainable commercial basis. Well-run crocodile farms which supply hides to the luxury leather trade are considered by many experts to be an acceptable way of exploiting crocodiles and alligators, because they minimise hunting in the wild. In parts of Africa farms breeding Nile crocodiles have certainly led to a reduction in poaching. Zambia is a good example where the government takes a fairly responsible attitude to crocodile farming. For several years the farms relied upon egg collecting from the wild until satisfactory breeding stocks were established. Wild strains are still sometimes introduced, to boost the strength of the stocks, but there is a levy on each egg collected and, once established, the farms are obliged to return a proportion of the eggs they hatch artificially to the wild.

Crocodile farms have become major tourist attractions in recent years and, although few commercial enterprises have been persuaded to cooperate, they could provide an opportunity to supply the public with up-to-date information on conservation and natural history.

Wildlife tourism

In the last 50 years tourism has become the fastest-growing industry on earth. It is an important source of revenue, particularly in many developing countries where the profusion of wildlife is one of the main attractions. People travel all over the world specifically to see certain animals: the roosting monarch butterflies in Mexico and California; the tigers at Ranthambhore in India; the bottlenose dolphins at Monkey Mia in Western Australia; the polar bears at Churchill in Canada; the seabird colonies on Heimaey in Iceland; the penguin colonies on the Falkland Islands; the sharks at feeding stations in the Maldives; the humpback whales off the coast of Newfoundland; and the lemurs in Madagascar.

At the same time, many countries rely almost entirely on their wildlife and wilderness areas to attract tourists. For example, most people visit Zambia to see the Victoria Falls; to participate in the famous walking safaris; to observe, photograph and hunt the wildlife; or to fish in some of the best tiger fishing grounds on the continent. Kenya is another good example where wildlife tourism is the principal foreign exchange earner in the country; in terms of visitor attraction, each lion in Amboseli National Park has been estimated to be worth some US$27,000 per year and each elephant herd an incredible US$610,000. This makes the animals worth considerably more alive than dead.

Admittedly, tourism is often a serious threat to wildlife and habitats and, so far, it has not been very conservation-minded. Over-commercialisation has taken its toll in many parts of the world – even some wilderness areas are well-manicured, with tarmac roads and more tourists than vultures around lion kills. But tourism can be developed in such a way that it meets the costs of conservation, without causing undue disturbance. It can also help with education: tourists who appreciate wildlife, and the importance and advantages of conservation, are more likely to accept it as a natural part of their daily lives. And it is a fact that if people can earn a living from wildlife they take an interest in its future. In this context, the great thing about tourism is that it is a benefit that will last indefinitely.

Besides, in many countries, if the government considers protecting wildlife at all, it insists that it must pay its own way. This is fine as long as the money made is not siphoned off and lost somewhere in government expenditures; it has to be ploughed back into conservation and used to help local communities so that they have a vested interest in protecting the wildlife or wild areas concerned.

A classic example is the mountain gorilla. Allowing tourists to visit mountain gorilla families has long been the subject of heated debate. Mountain gorillas are very rare animals, with only 100 survivors in Uganda's Impenetrable Forest and 280 in the Virunga Volcanoes region straddling the borders of Zaire, Rwanda and Uganda. The problem is that they are too rare to take any risks. However, the gorillas are demonstrating that wildlife can be a significant source of foreign exchange; this has become a major incentive for protecting them in Zaire and Rwanda, both of which are desperately hard-up.

There are two main areas of concern:

- That gorillas used to seeing people every day will lose their natural fear, making it easier for poachers to kill them.
- That there is a serious risk of them catching a disease to which they have no immunity.

But habituating the gorillas to people may actually be beneficial. They are relatively easy to kill anyway because, if approached closely, the dominant male silverback rushes up and confronts his attacker instead of running away. In addition, the poachers tend to avoid habituated groups because they know they are being followed by people every day.

The risk of disease is a calculated one. Mountain gorillas in Rwanda recently experienced an outbreak of a respiratory illness; they were coughing, their noses were constantly running and they lost weight. Between February and May 1988 six of the gorillas died and 27 recovered after treatment. A month later, another gorilla was found with measles and, using blow darts, the survivors had to be vaccinated immediately.

The aim of such management is to make as much money as possible while keeping disturbance and direct contact to a minimum. In Zaire, groups are limited to six tourists per visit, each paying US$100 for the privilege. During peak periods, in July and August, 90 per cent of the places are filled while, the year-round average is 55 per cent. Four of the 29 mountain gorilla families in the country have been habituated to tourists and these are already earning almost half a million dollars every year. With the popularity of the film *Gorillas in the Mist* they are likely to be earning almost twice as much in the near future.

WILDLIFE CASE STUDIES

There are certain wildlife conservation efforts that have attracted more attention than most; for example, elephants, rhinos, whales, dolphins and seals have been in the news constantly in recent years. Perhaps it is because the campaigns to save them have been conducted so publicly, or perhaps it is because we are only just beginning to realise that animals we have always taken for granted are vulnerable.

But in overall terms, with so many threatened species around the world, the larger and more exciting ones are just the tip of the iceberg. The plight of many other animals and, especially, plants rarely makes headline news. However, the publicity and awareness generated by the powerful conservation flagships ultimately will benefit all threatened species. The most disturbing fact is that the exciting animals themselves are proving so difficult to protect. For example, people have been warning of the dangers of overhunting whales since the 1930s yet, despite considerable progress, more than half a century later the whaling continues.

Wildlife conservation over such long periods of time requires perseverance and patience. It takes years to build up the pressure on decision-makers, using well-rehearsed argument and public support; and, in the meantime, the momentum of field conservation projects has to be maintained. But for many species time is running out and the challenge now is to speed up this conservation process.

African elephant poaching
Nearly 800,000 African elephants were killed by poachers in the 1980s. There are now no more than 600,000 left in the whole of Africa, while a much more pessimistic estimate puts the figure at 353,000. Yet despite the enormous sums of money now being spent on anti-poaching operations, the illegal killing continues.

Once found throughout most of Africa, except in extreme deserts, the elephant is now extinct or critically endangered in many countries. East Africa has been hit particularly hard; elephant populations in the region have crashed by more than 80 per cent since the early 1970s. Kenya alone has lost more than 100,000 elephants since 1973, the total number of survivors in the country today standing at no more than 16,000. In Tsavo, roughly the size of Wales, and Kenya's largest park, bleached white elephant bones and bloodied carcasses have become almost as common as the sight of live elephants.

In addition to the number of elephants being killed, there is also concern about the effect of the ivory trade on the family life of survivors. Elephants live in a complex and highly organised social world and their population structure and breeding patterns are probably being disrupted to such an extent that, even if the poaching stopped today, it could take 25 years for them to get back to normal.

Both males and females carry tusks, which are really just enlarged teeth. These tusks first appear when the animals are about two years old, and grow throughout their life; they are used mainly for feeding (prising bark from trees and digging for roots), but also function as weapons in social encounters. There are records of very old bulls with tusks weighing 125 kg and measuring more than 3.5 metres long, but half of all African elephants are killed before they are 15 years old – they have a potential lifespan in the wild of about 60 years – so nowadays long tusks are extremely rare. Indeed, mature elephants are so scarce that the poachers kill even the babies for their pathetic quantities of ivory. This is illustrated by some tragic statistics. A tonne of ivory in 1979 represented 54 dead elephants; by 1987 the same weight represented no fewer than 113, not counting the many calves that would have been orphaned and left to die of starvation.

Ivory has been harvested from many parts of Africa for more than five centuries, but in recent years the odds have been weighed heavily against the elephants. In the early 1960s Africa's political upheavals – civil wars, guerrilla campaigns and other conflicts – made semi-automatic and automatic weapons widely available. Then in the early 1970s the worldwide economic recession encouraged investors to switch to ivory as a wealth store. This caused a sudden increase in its value, and a wave of illegal hunting.

Killing the elephants is easy – an entire herd can be machine-gunned down in a matter of seconds. Alternatively, the poachers simply kill one animal and wait; the social bonds between elephants are so strong that, if one member of a herd is shot, the others will often come to its aid, even in the face of considerable danger. It is an unfortunate behaviour pattern that plays straight into the hands of the poachers.

Raw ivory prices have risen 30-fold since the 1960s from roughly £3 per kilo in the late 1960s to over £100 per kilo in the early 1990s. The poachers themselves, of course, are paid a tiny fraction of the real value of the ivory they collect, but they are desperate people and need whatever money they can get. And it is a violent business. In some countries, poachers are so determined that they will kill anyone who stands in their way. Three tourists were shot by poachers in July 1989 as they stumbled upon gangs at work in a Kenyan park. The poachers are certainly willing to kill park rangers and wardens to achieve their aims.

Kenya has therefore been forced to deploy army helicopter

gunships in a last-ditch effort to save its dwindling elephant herds. It is one of the many African states that shoots poachers on sight – nearly 100 were killed in one recent ten-month period. In contrast, Zambia's anti-poaching patrols cannot fire at the poachers except in self-defence, although the authorities are considering training their staff in new anti-terrorist skills and tactics with which to fight back. In the meantime, they are provided only with hunting rifles and expected to tackle determined and dangerous gangs of professional poachers equipped with sophisticated radio communications equipment and armed with a range of automatic weapons. Many of these gangs use Kalashnikov AK47s left over from the days when Zambia hosted guerrillas fighting in Zimbabwe. The scouts have no legal rights in shoot-outs with poachers – which occur frequently – yet there may be only five of them trying to arrest a gang of more than 30.

The areas the anti-poaching patrols have to protect are enormous. Garamba National Park in north-eastern Zaire covers an area of 5,000 square kilometres of long-grass savanna which is very difficult terrain to work in. The Park has a total of 246 trained staff, but only 58 men are available for active patrol duties, and they have to cover this vast area on foot.

Despite the difficult conditions, anti-poaching patrol scouts are usually dedicated men and surprisingly successful. In Garamba, before there was an efficient anti-poaching operation to tackle the large gangs of poachers from both Zaire and across the border in Sudan, the Park's elephant population declined from 22,000 in 1976 to about 4,000 ten years later. Since then the operation has been working more efficiently so that today there are more than 5,000 of the animals and the numbers are continuing to rise slowly. Park staff were delighted in April 1988 when an enormous herd of 800 elephants was spotted during a routine anti-poaching operation.

In Zambia's Luangwa Valley, where poachers have killed 75,000 elephants since the 1970s, the patrols have made nearly 2,000 arrests, impounded hundreds of firearms and confiscated more than 1,500 elephant tusks and dozens of rhino horns. And on 17 July 1989 the Kenyan Government ceremoniously burned about 12 tonnes of raw ivory which had been recovered from poachers over the previous five years.

The world's biggest-ever ivory cache was found in Namibia in September 1989 when police managed to break a massive international smuggling syndicate, capturing 25 people with 980 tusks weighing about 7 tonnes.

But anti-poaching operations of this kind, while necessary, clearly are not getting to the core of the problem. The ivory trade is big business and has been worth as much as £250 million a year, though recently its value has dropped to nearer £30 million. The opportunity to obtain hard currency through the trade has even tempted many diplomats and politicians in Africa to organise or help in the illegal smuggling operations. While there is still demand for ivory – the tusks are carved into ornaments, or made into piano keys, chopsticks, billiard balls and other goods – international smugglers will continue to find loopholes in the law.

The trade is controlled by the CITES Convention, so that, until recently, three-quarters of the ivory was being sold on the black market, with the remaining quarter being traded quite legally. However elephants are now listed on Appendix I of CITES, which effectively bans all commercial trade in their products between signatory countries. The ban came into force on 18 January 1990, and the United States, the European Community and Japan – the three main ivory markets – had already imposed immediate trade bans of their own. The Japanese move was particularly surprising and encouraging, welcomed by conservationists who had long regarded Japan as an intransigent nation on many wildlife trade issues.

But legal ivory is still on the world market, for two reasons. Firstly, non-signatories to CITES, such as South Korea and several countries in the Middle East, are not bound by its decisions. Secondly, CITES has a system whereby any party can exempt itself from a ban by taking out a 'reservation' within a 90-day 'grace' period. Reservations were registered by seven countries – Britain (for a six-month period), South Africa, Botswana, Malawi, Zimbabwe, Zambia and China – enabling them all to continue selling and exporting ivory quite legitimately. Britain's decision in particular appalled the conservationists of the world. Its interest in taking out a reservation was in 500 tonnes of ivory, worth millions of pounds, which was stockpiled in Hong Kong at the time of the ban, but releasing this huge quantity into the trade will stimulate demand in new markets, going against the whole strategy of the ivory ban. It may also have the effect of encouraging further smuggling. The British government says that the exemption is only for six months in order to allow the 'legal' stocks of ivory to be run down and to allow time for retraining of the carvers in the ivory business. Yet the carvers' union in Hong Kong has admitted that nearly 80 per cent of its carvers have found new jobs already.

Several of the other countries opting for reservations had an entirely different reason for refusing to comply. Although elephants are seriously threatened throughout most of their range, in a few countries in southern Africa their populations are stable or even rising. For years limited numbers of these animals have been culled – and their ivory sold – quite legally. Zimbabwe, in particular, was very angry with the Appendix I listing and felt that it was being penalised by the ban for the management failures elsewhere in Africa. In the early days of British colonisation in the country (then Southern Rhodesia), excessive hunting had reduced Zimbabwe's elephant population to fewer than 4,000. But stringent conservation measures and careful management have encouraged their numbers to increase dramatically and there is now a thriving population of more than 52,000. But there has been a price to pay. The elephants must earn their keep and are managed as an important foreign exchange earner, with a designated number (from 1,200 to 5,300 in the 1980s) being killed each year. Some of these are allotted to safari hunters – a surprising number of people are prepared to pay thousands of pounds each for the pleasure of killing an elephant. Nevertheless, their contribution is a lucrative part of the business.

Very little of a culled animal goes to waste. Its ivory and hide fetch good prices at government auctions; it provides large quantities of meat; its skin is tanned and used for leather goods; and even its fat can be used for cooking oil. At the end of the day, each dead elephant can be worth in excess of £15,000. Many of the proceeds go to local farmers, who put up with elephants trespassing on their land only because of this financial compensation. The money can also be used to pay local people to act as guides, and to cover the costs of game wardens who supervise the cull and keep the poachers out. The culling programme is strictly controlled by the government, which also considers it important because too many elephants in restricted areas (such as national parks) tend to damage their own woodland homes.

A compromise for the southern African states was proposed at the most recent CITES meeting. If they were to accept a trading moratorium in the short-term (lasting long enough to break the back of the international poaching community) then a limited trade in ivory, based on strictly-controlled culling programmes, might possibly work in the longer-term. But this proposal has split the world's conservationists into two bitterly opposed camps.

On the one hand, many experts argue that managing elephants as an exploitable resource is repugnant and that killing them should not be allowed under any circumstances. They also point out that live elephants can be worth more than dead ones, since they are one of the animals most visitors to Africa long to see. And they claim that the southern African states are profoundly involved in trafficking contraband and distorting the truth. But their greatest concern is that, with current inadequate controls, the existence of any legal trade in ivory makes it harder, or even impossible, to stop smuggling; it simply allows poachers to continue to launder illegal ivory.

Other experts would prefer to see a limited, tightly controlled trade. They say that there will always be a demand for ivory, irrespective of whether it is available legally or only on the black market. And they are concerned that, if elephant ivory is not available, the traders and carvers may turn for their needs to other animal products, such as hippopotamus teeth or the tusks of walruses, narwals and warthogs. As if to prove this last point, a group of ivory carvers in West Germany is now negotiating with the geological ministry in Moscow for mammoth tusks discovered along the coast of the Laptev Sea and elsewhere on the Siberian tundra. It has been illegal to import elephant ivory into West Germany since June 1989 and the carvers are facing unemployment. They say that the mammoth tusks, preserved for up to 20,000 years in the permafrost, are easier to polish than elephant ivory. If they are granted permission, there is concern that a consignment of tusks labelled 'mammoth ivory' could contain 90 per cent elephant ivory, and it would be difficult for customs officials to tell the difference.

Above all, the pro-trade lobby argues that the Zimbabwe culling programme is an enlightened form of conservation – a prime example of how wildlife utilisation can protect species and benefit people at the same time. The core of the poaching problem has always been that the interests of an individual generally differ from those of society at large. An individual is more likely to kill as many elephants as possible, even at the risk of driving the species to extinction. What Zimbabwe has done is to bring their long-term value to society more closely in line with the individual pay-offs from poaching; in other words, local people are being rewarded financially for conserving elephants. It is certainly a more efficient use of elephants than poaching, where the tusks are hacked out with machetes and the carcasses left to rot.

Whatever the arguments about culling and trade, the current situation is totally unacceptable. Past experience has shown that, as soon as one ivory smuggling channel is blocked, another is opened up almost immediately. Elephant poaching is being organised efficiently by master-criminal syndicates with access to sophisticated techniques, and if there are any loopholes at all they will find them.

Therefore the southern African ivory trading cartel, which

sidesteps the CITES agreement, undermines international efforts to save the elephant because there is no longer the full cooperation of every country concerned. To shut down the ivory trade effectively requires unprecedented international political will and cooperation.

While the legal wrangling continues, the problem is being tackled on two fronts:

- With an international campaign to sway public opinion.
- With field operations to capture the poachers and smugglers red-handed.

However, it all costs money. WWF alone is spending £1.5 million in 1990 on elephant projects in eight countries. With several other conservation bodies, it has prepared an Elephant Action Plan and it is possible that wealthy countries may yet put up some of the substantial sums required to implement it. But time is running out. It has been estimated that only 44,000 elephants (across just 2 per cent of the species' range) are currently receiving effective protection. If the present level of poaching continues, no other elephants in Africa are likely to survive.

Rhino poaching

There were 70,000 rhinos in the world in 1970; today, in 1990, there are fewer than 11,000 left. There are two species in Africa and three in Asia, but only one of them can be considered at all safe. Rhinos are being hunted to the point of extinction for their horns. As one expert has commented 'To kill a two and a half ton rhino merely to cut off its horn is like destroying a cathedral in order to steal the cross from its spire.'

Rhino horn is not a horn in the conventional sense because, unlike the horns of most other animals, it is not bony. Mounted on a roughened knob on the skull, it is made of a fibrous protein called keratin, which grows from the animal's skin. It keeps growing throughout the rhino's life, by several inches every year; one record-holder had a horn which measured nearly 2 metres long. If it is accidentally broken off, a new one will grow in its place.

Rhinos use their horns for 'wrestling', a kind of ritualised conflict that is designed to permit a trial of strength while minimising the risk of injury. It doesn't always work, as the males sometimes fight viciously and inflict gaping wounds. The horns are also used to defend the youngsters against powerful enemies, such as lions or crocodiles, and even just to clear the way ahead as the rhinos walk, head down, along tangled paths. Some species also cross horns with one another during courtship.

No trade in rhino horn is allowed. And with the sole exception of southern white rhinos in South Africa, which can be hunted with a special licence, they are legally protected everywhere. There has never been much demand for the horns in Africa itself, but they continue to be smuggled out of the continent (and all over Asia) for sale on the black market. Many countries are involved in this illegal trade, some because they have wild rhino populations but many others because they act as distribution centres or consumers.

More than half the horn goes to the small Arabian country of North Yemen, where it has been used for over 1,000 years to make so-called *jambiyya* dagger handles. The daggers are made by experienced craftsmen and worn by virtually every adult man in the country. They are status symbols, signifying that the wearers are capable of defending themselves; and it is believed that the precise choice of handle depends upon the owner's social class. Virtually all the horn used in Yemen is from African rhinos, although the fact that it comes from rhinos at all appears to be immaterial. They have no special significance to the people of North Yemen; rhino horn is preferred to other materials simply because it improves with age and handling, and because it increases in value – some daggers are thought to be worth hundreds of thousands of pounds.

North Yemen banned the import of rhino horn in 1982, but for several years afterwards demand for it in the country continued to increase dramatically as the oil wealth of the region made people richer. Attitudes are changing slowly, however, and many young men today are not so interested in the traditions of their fathers and grandfathers. There is still a high demand for rhino horn, particularly as a safe form of investment, but the amount entering the country actually decreased in the late 1980s.

The remainder of the horn on the international market is sold mainly in the Far East, for use in traditional medicines (which also use rhino nails, hooves, blood, urine and hides). Contrary to popular belief, less than 1 per cent is used as an aphrodisiac, and then only in parts of north India. Traditional rhino horn medicines are particularly popular in Taiwan; the horn is ground into a powder and turned into hundreds of different potions, used as fever-reducing agents, and to treat headaches, various skin diseases, toothache, heart and liver trouble, measles, nosebleeds and even snake bites. Many scientists doubt whether any of these potions really work and consider rhino horn to be nothing more than an expensive placebo. Chemically, there is nothing unique about it – keratin is a major ingredient of our own hair and nails, as well as of feathers, beaks and scales. But millions of people do believe in the medicinal value of rhino horn, and they are willing to pay large sums of money for it. African horn costs about £3.50 per gram, but in Taiwan horn from Indian and Sumatran rhinos can fetch up to £28 per gram, and demand is decreasing in Singapore and Hong Kong as the Chinese there become more westernised. However, in some parts of Asia businessmen are buying the horns as an investment, believing that the animals will soon disappear from the wild; the rarer rhinos become, the higher the value of their horns and the greater the demand.

The rarest – and paradoxically the commonest – of all the rhinos is the white rhino. There are two varieties, which look almost identical, and both have two horns, making them doubly attractive to poachers. But their genetic differences are so great, having lived apart for some two million years, that scientists consider them to be separate sub-species.

Northern white rhinos were first discovered by western scientists in 1903. At the time they were common in Chad, Central African Republic, Sudan, Uganda and Zaire. By 1984 the population had plummeted. There were two unconfirmed sightings in Southern National Park, Sudan, but the only positive reports were of just 15 animals, all living in Zaire's Garamba National Park. In May that year poachers killed two more and the population was down to an all-time low of 13, with a further 12 in captivity. But no more have been killed since, thanks to a major anti-poaching effort. Indeed, there have been several births and, with no fewer than three babies being born in the Park during 1989, the total population has now risen to 25. Clearly, the northern white rhino is still in a terribly precarious position, but experience with its closest relative, the southern white, gives some cause for hope.

The southern white rhino was considered to be extinct as long ago as 1882, but at the turn of the century a small population of 11 animals was discovered in Umfolozi, Zululand. This prompted an extraordinary effort to save them from extinction and, by the mid-1960s, the numbers had increased to about 500. A programme was then devised to split the population up, and they were transferred to parks and reserves in other countries. There are now more than 5,000 of them throughout southern Africa, and they are out of immediate danger.

Unfortunately, the same cannot be said of the other African species, the black rhino which, of all five members of the family, is under the most pressure from the illegal trade. It is actually no more black than the white rhinos are white – they are all a grey-brown colour. It also has two horns in tandem, although they are usually a little shorter. Once widespread in all suitable habitats over most of Africa south of the Sahara, black rhinos are currently being killed at a faster rate than anyone thought possible 20 years ago. In the 1980s the numbers declined by a staggering 93 per cent in Tanzania, 96 per cent in Zambia and 99 per cent in Kenya. The total population in Africa has crashed from 65,000 in 1970 to fewer than 3,500 today.

The three Asian rhinos are also in serious danger, after suffering a massive reduction in numbers, and a considerable contraction of their ranges, last century. Their horns are considerably smaller than those on African rhinos, and not as sharply pointed, but for a long time have been in great local demand along with almost all the rhinos' other organs. The rarest of the three is the Javan rhino which, until the middle of the 19th century, was widespread in south-east Asia from India and China southwards to Indonesia. By the 1930s it was extinct everywhere except the Udjung Kulon Reserve in western Java, although there continue to be scattered, but unconfirmed, reports of them along the Thai/Burmese border. There are fewer than 70 survivors altogether. The Sumatran rhino was also found over much of south-east Asia; often called the hairy rhino, because of the coarse hairs on its skin, its population has been reduced to about 750 animals scattered throughout parts of Indonesia, Malaysia, Thailand, Laos, Kampuchea and Burma.

The Indian rhino, which has a rather prehistoric appearance and looks as if it is armour-plated, was once widespread in Pakistan, India, Nepal, Bhutan and Bangladesh, but today there are no more than 1,700 survivors, restricted to a few reserves in India and Nepal. More than three-quarters of them live in Kaziranga and Chitwan National Parks. Poaching is still a chronic problem, although it appears to be declining due largely to the efforts of Park staff; in Kaziranga, 41 rhinos were killed in 1986 but 'only' 24 in 1987. They are now suffering from competition with domestic animals grazing within these reserves and, particularly in Kaziranga, increasing flood levels. The highest floods ever recorded were in 1988, causing the deaths of at least 38 Indian rhinos.

Simple-minded and ponderous creatures, with poor eyesight, rhinos are ill-equipped to cope with poachers armed with modern weapons. They are difficult animals to protect. Banning the trade has not worked, although it may well have reduced the scale of the slaughter. There will always be people willing to risk poaching or smuggling while the demand for rhino horn still exists. And there will always be ways of getting the horns across national borders; a bribe of less than £50 is apparently enough to make a customs officer turn a blind eye when smuggling rhino products into Taiwan. Meanwhile, anti-poaching efforts in the field have been hampered by wars, revolutions, civil disturbances and, in particular, by a lack of resources to combat poachers on their own terms.

A lack of human and financial resources has always been a major problem. Some conservationists would like to be able to sell the horns they confiscate from poachers, in order to raise money for their anti-poaching operations. It must be frustrating to be sitting on millions of pounds worth of horns when money is desperately needed to save surviving rhinos. But many experts believe that lifting the ban may stimulate demand and raise the value of the horn even higher.

Another controversial idea is to make the rhinos worthless to poachers by removing the horns under anaesthetic. It is an idea that has been tossed around at conservation meetings in Africa for many years, but it is fraught with difficulties. De-horning is relatively inexpensive but, because the horns re-grow, has to be repeated at frequent intervals. There is also a risk that poachers will kill the animals anyway, in the mistaken belief that there might be a small piece of horn left. The idea sounds rather drastic and, although removing the horn is synonymous with removing a fingernail rather than the finger itself, no one really knows if rhinos can live without it. However, a de-horning operation is being attempted on the fringes of the Namib desert in north-western Namibia, in a desperate bid to save the last of the black rhinos there. The poachers use razor-sharp pangas, but conservationists neatly saw the horns off before filing them down to neat stumps. So far, after more than a year, it has proved successful; no rhinos have died from the operations themselves, and none have been killed by poachers.

The relocation of rhinos to areas where they can more easily be protected is being attempted in several areas, including India; round-the-clock protection by armed guards in special enclosures is another, and more drastic, alternative. The latter is time-consuming and expensive, and many people dislike the idea of taking away the rhinos' freedom, but it is considered by many to be a major improvement on conventional anti-poaching operations, which are forced to spread their limited resources over vast areas of land. The animals are captured and moved to special fenced enclosures within national parks. Several high-security rhino sanctuaries of this kind have been established in Kenya, including one at Lake Nakuru National Park. A number of rhinos have been released in the Park, which now has 80 kilometres of electric fencing around its perimeter, to join two which were previously resident there, the aim being to build up the population to a point where animals can be reintroduced into some of their old haunts.

The rhinos are certainly safer in semi-captivity than they were roaming free, but not entirely safe. For example, there used to be five white rhinos under constant armed guard in Kenya's Meru National Park, but one night in October 1988 30 well-armed Somali poachers attacked the park headquarters and held the rangers at bay while they killed all five animals and removed their horns.

More strenuous efforts to stem the international trade in rhino horn are also urgently needed. There is no single project that will end the demand or tighten the controls, but there are several promising avenues of attack. Finding acceptable alternatives to rhino horn is of paramount importance. In some parts of the world water buffalo or saiga antelope horn, which are incomparably cheaper, are traditionally acceptable medicinal substitutes. If rhino horn can be taken off the shelves it will be forgotten – once swallowed, it has gone forever.

But in North Yemen there will always be an interest in rhino horns because the daggers are passed from generation to generation as family heirlooms, and will therefore always be around. However high quality synthetic materials might satisfy at least some of the future demand, even if it could not solve the investment problem. The government of North Yemen is attempting to discourage the use of rhino horn, but there is no wildlife conservation organisation in the country to support its efforts. No one there appears to realise that the rhino is in danger of extinction, so an educational programme could be very beneficial.

The situation is so desperate that drastic, and at times unpopular, measures are now the only hope for the world's rhinos – or we could be left with literally nothing to save.

Whaling

All commercial whaling has been officially banned since October 1985, but the ban exists on paper only – more than 12,000 whales have been slaughtered since it came into effect. This is typical of the whaling industry, which has repeatedly ignored international regulations. One by one, whale species have plunged to less than 2 per cent of their original population levels – almost to the point of extinction.

Commercial whaling has always focused on the largest and most profitable species – the great whales. There are ten different great whales – the blue, fin, humpback, right, bowhead (or Greenland), Bryde's, sei, minke, grey and sperm whales. But most of these are now commercially extinct and several could ultimately disappear altogether.

Coastal communities have probably killed whales since time immemorial; they would certainly have taken advantage of dead whales washed ashore, using the blubber for light and heat, and the meat as a welcome source of food. So it is not hard to imagine how this might have developed into some kind of subsistence hunting, since whales would have made tempting targets within easy reach of coastal people; several whale species hug the coastline and they all have to come to the surface to breathe.

Commercial whaling probably began with the Basques, in the Bay of Biscay, under 1,000 years ago. Entire villages cooperated when a whale was sighted from the shore. They used small rowing boats (which had to be taken to within a few metres of the whales) and hand-held harpoons. Once the whale was killed and brought ashore the blubber was boiled down in large open pots to provide oil for lighting or to make soap; the tongues were considered a delicacy, but there was little interest in the meat.

By the 18th and 19th centuries whaling had become big business. The English, Dutch, Americans, Japanese and other nations had their own whaling fleets and were making enormous profits. The more effort they put into the industry, the more money they could make. This quickly resulted in several technological developments which spelt disaster for the whales. The first came in 1864 when a Norwegian named Svend Foyn developed the explosive harpoon which can be fired from a cannon. The harpoon consists of a pole (attached to a line) with a barbed head. Screwed into the head is a grenade, consisting of a detonator and a sack of black gunpowder in a steel container equipped with spikes. The harpoon is aimed immediately in front of the whale's flippers so that it enters either the lungs, heart or spinal region; two or three seconds then elapse from the time the harpoon hits the whale to when the grenade explodes inside its body. This awful weapon precipitated an enormous increase in whaling worldwide and, even though the whale is rarely killed outright, it is still in use today. Foyn also invented a hollow spear that enabled the whalers to pump their quarry full of air. This kept the animals afloat while they were towed back to shore for processing.

But the need to return to shore-based stations with the catches was considered to be a major limitation on the potential of the whaling industry. The next dramatic development, in the early 1920s, solved this problem. It was the introduction of floating factory ships with slipways to winch the whales up for processing on board. These were designed to accompany fleets of catcher boats which, by this time, were being built with enough speed to catch even the swiftest of whales. Later still, the boats were fitted with the most sophisticated tracking equipment from which the whales could not hide.

Whale numbers have decreased dramatically during the last 300 years, with one population being wiped out after another. As one species became rarer, attention turned to another, and then another, and so on. Bowhead whales were considered one of the most valuable because of the thickness of their blubber, but were too rare to be of any economic importance by 1900. Hunting of sperm whales began in 1712; at one time, there were 600 American ships hunting them in the Atlantic and as many as 30,000 were killed in some years. By the 1920s the Atlantic sperm whale population was practically extinct.

It was around this time that the whalers turned their attentions to the Antarctic waters which, until the beginning of the century, had not been touched. There were about a quarter of a million blue whales there at the time; today, there are between 200 and 1,100 left.

There have been a number of attempts to control whaling over the years, but the majority of these were to protect national interests rather than the whales themselves. Effectively, until the early 1930s, whaling was an uncontrolled free-for-all; anyone could kill as many whales as they liked, and how they liked. Then, in 1931, the Convention for the Regulation of Whaling was drawn up. By that time grey, bowhead and right whales were virtually extinct and several others were in serious trouble. But the Convention barely scratched the surface of the whaling issue; it protected bowhead and right whales but made no attempt to restrict the numbers of whales of other species being killed; and, besides, five major whaling nations had refused to accede to it.

One of the concepts introduced by the Convention was something called the blue whale unit (BWU). It was a measure that lumped all great whales together, regardless of species – one BWU equalled one blue whale, or two fin, three humpback, five sei and so on. Since it was more profitable to fulfill a quota with a few large whales than many smaller ones, the immediate result was a mad scramble for blue whales, the largest animals ever to have lived on earth.

Then in 1946 the Convention was replaced with the so-called Whaling Convention, which has overseen the world's whaling activities ever since. It has mixed objectives, established to protect whales as well as to encourage the development of the whaling industry. The Convention established a body called the International Whaling Commission (IWC) which meets every year to discuss and adopt regulations on catch quotas, protected species and whaling methods. Its role in life is effectively to manage the world's whales for sustainable exploitation.

Initially the IWC was a pathetic shambles. Its members were the whalers themselves – it was dubbed the whalers' club – and they worked on the basis of gentlemen's agreements, all of which were broken on numerous occasions. Scientists' recommendations were ignored and the number of whales being killed actually increased, reaching an all-time peak of 64,000 in the 1960–1 season. In desperation, at the United Nations Conference on the Environment in 1972, the UN voted overwhelmingly for a ten-year moratorium; it was passed by 53 votes to nought, with 12 abstentions. However the IWC was unmoved, and ignored the plea, although in the same year it did finally abandon the use of BWUs. Gradually though, in the face of increasing public outrage, the IWC began to change. It reduced catch quotas, established its own scientific committee, accepted many more (non-whaling) members and eventually began to treat each stock of each species separately.

But the IWC still does not work properly. When the hard-line whalers are determined to do something there is basically nothing to stop them and, for many years, efforts to save the whales have constantly been taking three steps forwards and two-and-a-half steps backwards.

Then in 1982 the IWC voted for an indefinite moratorium of not less than five years, to begin in 1985. It was hailed as a great victory by the conservationists, and many countries (including Britain, the United States and Australia) welcomed the decision. But the IWC is notorious for behind-the-scenes bribery, blackmail and sleazy dealings. It was even rumoured, in the late 1970s, that Panama had been forced to withdraw an earlier proposal for a whaling moratorium when the Japanese threatened to renege on a deal worth $9.75 million to finance a new sugar refinery in the country. And the general rule is that, if a loophole can be found, it will be used to avoid unpopular IWC regulations. During the late 1970s and early 1980s, for example, pirate whaling fleets were set up under flags of convenience, such as Somalia and Liechtenstein, specifically to operate outside the IWC.

Needless to say, the commercial whaling ban has not worked. The IWC itself has no way of enforcing any of its regulations and it was totally ignored or circumvented by a number of countries. At the time of writing, Japan, Norway and Iceland are still whaling in defiance of this world peace treaty with the whales. In 1989 alone they killed, between them, 270 minke, 68 fin and 10 sei whales. They have claimed that their whaling is for 'scientific purposes', this serious loophole in the regulations allowing any nation to issue its own permits to take any number of whales for scientific research – even though the whales are still allowed to be processed for their meat and oil in the normal way. Whaling under this guise is dismissed as a sham by the world's conservationists and even the IWC's own scientific committee has condemned it, saying that it will add nothing to our knowledge about the animals. The main aim for the whalers is to avoid having to close down their commercial whaling operations until they can find a way of lifting the current moratorium.

But there are two amendments in American fisheries law designed specifically to give the IWC regulations more teeth. These enable the United States government to take action against any country which diminishes the effectiveness of the IWC, by denying them access to fish within its waters or by blocking imports of fisheries products. In theory it is an excellent idea: in reality it is hampered by a variety of political pressures.

The amendments have been used in the past, but not when they were most needed. Indeed, in 1984–5 a consortium of conservation organisations took legal action against the Commerce and State Departments to prevent an under-the-table deal with Japan; they were concerned that the United States would try to avoid imposing sanctions against Japan, which was planning a large sperm whale hunt after the species had officially been protected. The case eventually went to the Supreme Court in 1986, where the conservationists lost. Meanwhile, the Japanese had caught their 400 sperm whales.

But campaigns by conservation organisations undoubtedly do put pressure on IWC members. According to Greenpeace, during a boycott in 1988–9 Iceland's fishing industry lost £30 million in cancelled orders. The boycott was finally called off late in 1989 when Iceland, under considerable international pressure, announced that it would abandon scientific whaling. At the time of writing, it seems possible that Japan and Norway will follow suit.

But it is unlikely that any of these countries intends to stop whaling altogether. They have already attempted to construct a case for 'small-type coastal whaling'. Their argument is that it would be indistinguishable from aboriginal subsistence whaling, which is still allowed in St Vincent and parts of Alaska, Canada, Greenland and Siberia. At the IWC meeting in 1989 the Japanese Commissioner made a protracted and impassioned plea for coastal communities in Japan to be permitted to kill 320 minke whales. He claimed that the people living in these areas were suffering unfair hardship due to the whaling moratorium. But his arguments did not hold true. An independent report by a Japanese conservation organisation showed that many of the boats that would be used are actually owned and operated by the large commercial whaling companies and that the financial contribution from whaling was insignificant to the people's economy – it would have been commercial whaling under yet another name and, fortunately, the Japanese were refused permission. But their response was astonishing. They threatened to kill thousands of smaller Dall's porpoises and Baird's beaked whales instead, both of which are outside the jurisdiction of the IWC. It was akin to hostage taking, and there was little anyone could do.

The Icelanders have also taken up the cudgels by announcing that there are more minke whales in their coastal waters than they once thought. They are keen to catch some of the 'surplus', claiming that the animals are eating all 'their' fish.

Assessing the status of whale populations has always been one of the greatest sources of controversy within the IWC. It is extremely difficult to count whales, and methods used in the 1960s and 1970s are now known to have been quite unreliable. The whalers have always used the highest estimates, while the conservationists have used the lowest. There is still no perfect technique, so the safest solution must be to give the benefit of doubt to the whales – particularly since they reproduce very slowly and their populations take ages to recover, if they are able to recover at all. The need for this approach was strongly enforced in a report released by the Scientific Committee of the IWC on the first day of its 1989 conference. The report sent a shock wave through the proceedings, announcing that previous population estimates had been substantially wrong; it concluded that there are far fewer surviving whales than anyone had previously thought and the implication is that several species are now in very serious trouble.

The degree of insensitivity of the whaling nations to this kind of news is astonishing. The whaling industry is certainly in crisis, but the governments of whaling nations do not want to be seen bowing to world pressure. It is an absurd situation and, in recent years, public opinion has swung from indifference to outrage at the thought of whales suffering because of politics. After all, the whales do not 'belong' only to Japan, Iceland and Norway. And it is not as if whaling makes an important contribution to their economies, or as if whale meat is an important source of protein. It is a delicacy – sold in Japan restaurants for £30 a kilogram – and relatively few people are employed in the industry. There are even artificial ways of making whale products such as candlewax, fertilisers, fish bait, drum skins, lipstick and pet food.

Above all, the moral argument for protecting whales is possibly stronger than for any other wildlife conservation issue. President George Bush captured the feelings of many people when he said 'whales have become symbolic of all the wildlife and precious natural resources that current environmental problems challenge us to support'.

The challenge continues with the IWC meeting in July 1990, at which the whaling moratorium is being reviewed. We have not yet driven any of the great whale species to extinction (despite killing 1.25 million of them) but, unless the moratorium is extended and properly enforced, it may happen yet. Meanwhile, the huge 23,000-tonne Japanese factory ship, accompanied by its three catcher boats, is yet again ploughing Antarctic waters for minke whales.

Dolphins and porpoises

River dolphins receive a certain amount of protection under national legislation, but the Yangtze river dolphin and others face extinction in the near future unless present trends of habitat degradation and illegal hunting can be halted and reversed. Marine dolphins and porpoises are also threatened by hunting and, on an even greater scale, by accidental drownings during a variety of fishing operations. But they do not receive any form of international protection. There is no control on how many are killed or how they are killed, even though some populations could be in serious trouble.

One notorious hunt takes place every year in the Faeroe Islands, in the north-east Atlantic between Iceland and Scotland. Long-finned pilot whales have been killed by the Faeroese for centuries. Jet black, and about 6 metres long, they are friendly and gregarious animals, and make easy prey, pods of 200 or more regularly swimming very close to the Faeroese shoreline. The hunts are announced by special bonfires, which bring together large numbers of islanders and their motor-powered fishing boats. Throwing stones, beating saucepans, shouting and yelling, everyone drives the whales into bays, until they are in shallow water. Then they hold the frightened animals with gaffs (barbed hooks on the end of long poles) and cut behind their blowholes with knives. Many of the hunters are unskilled, or drunk, and use nothing more than penknives. Few of the whales are killed outright; some thrash about in pain so violently that they snap their spines.

The Faeroes is self-governing, and has its own language and currency, but belongs to Denmark. It has a total population of some 46,000 people, inhabiting five of the 23 islands in the group. It was once a poor, struggling nation and relied on whale meat as an important source of food. But nowadays the Faeroese prime minister boasts that his country has one of the highest standards of living in the world. A 320-kilometre exclusive economic zone around the group has boosted fish exports (mostly to Britain and the United States) and means that everyone can now afford a wide variety of food, fashionable clothes, new cars and many other luxury goods. This makes the claim that the islanders still need to kill pilot whales for food rather unconvincing. They continue to eat whale meat (on average, one meal a week) but tend to cut only prime steaks from the dead animals. Indeed, there have been many reports of piles of meat and carcasses being dumped on the local rubbish tips.

At least 230,000 pilot whales have been killed in the hunt since records began in 1709, with an annual peak of 2,973 in 1981. But it is not only pilot whales that are being killed. Any species which happens to be passing gets caught up in the hunt. In 1988, in addition to 1,690 pilot whales, the islanders also slaughtered 600 white-sided dolphins, three bottlenose whales and one killer whale. In 1989 they killed 1,258 pilot whales and unknown numbers of other species.

Calls to stop the hunt have been ignored by the Faeroese for years. Although no longer necessary, it is an old tradition that many of the islanders enjoy celebrating. But more than anything else, like whaling in other nations, it has become a matter of principle, and the Faeroese have no intention of bowing to international pressure.

Dolphins are hunted commercially by several countries, including Taiwan, Sri Lanka, Japan and Peru. The collapse of the anchoveta fishery in Peru (which was once the largest fishery in the world) left thousands of men out of work and encouraged them to use their nets to catch dolphins. More than 10,000 dusky dolphins and, since 1987, increasing numbers of common dolphins, are now taken annually for sale in the local markets, and there are signs that the industry is growing rapidly.

The Japanese use the same shore-drive fishery technique as the Faeroese do for pilot whales. In this way they kill thousands of false killer whales, short-finned pilot whales, striped dolphins, spotted dolphins, bottlenose dolphins and common dolphins. They also employ small whaling vessels, equipped with harpoon guns, to hunt short-finned pilot whales and Baird's beaked whales. And smaller boats are used to take Dall's porpoises, and several other species, with hand-held harpoons. There is grave concern that demand for dolphin meat in Japan will increase as supplies of whale meat decline; it is usually sold as a delicacy for the expensive end of the market, rarely for local consumption. Some of the hunts are already quite large and populations of several species in Japanese waters appear to be threatened.

In Chile dolphins and porpoises are used as bait for crab fishing; more than 5,000 black dolphins, Commerson's dolphins and Burmeister's porpoises are harpooned or shot every year for this purpose, as well as fur seals, sealions, penguins and other wildlife. The Chilean crab fishery began 60 years ago but is now highly profitable and expanding rapidly; it has grown by 500 per cent in the 1980s, with most of the crab being exported as an internationally-prized seafood delicacy. The fishermen are supposed to use mutton, which is the official crab bait, but dolphin meat is much cheaper and lasts for longer in the water. They call the dolphins *tontitas*, or 'silly ones', because they are so friendly and easy to kill; if the fishermen manage to injure one animal, the others will come to its rescue, despite the danger to themselves.

Fishermen in many parts of the world consider dolphins and porpoises to be undesirable competitors, and sometimes kill them for threatening fish stocks. For example, in the late 1970s Norway hunted 327 killer whales (the largest members of the dolphin family) which were believed to be preventing the recovery of herring stocks in its coastal waters.

But incidental catches of dolphins and porpoises during fishing operations are a more important threat. Every year hundreds of thousands of dolphins and porpoises are caught (and drowned) accidentally in fishing nets all over the world. Gill-nets in the Gulf of California drown large numbers of vaquita, a kind of harbour porpoise endemic to the area; similar nets kill Hector's dolphins, which are endemic to the coastal waters of New Zealand; and they kill spinner and bottlenose dolphins off the coasts of India. Even the rarest member of the family, the Chinese Yangtze river dolphin, gets entangled in fishing lines and hooks; there may be as few as 200 of these animals left, so even small catches are significant.

Tuna fishing, predominantly in the Pacific Ocean, is considered the most serious problem facing marine species. Yellowfin and skipjack tuna tend to follow dolphins to good feeding grounds and the two animals are often found together. When the fishermen find a school of dolphins, they deliberately set their huge nets around them in the hope of catching the tuna as well. In the eastern tropical Pacific alone, some 800 boats set 48,000 kilometres of nylon driftnets each night – more than enough to circle the earth at the equator. Each net is up to 48 kilometres long and hangs like a curtain to a depth of 15–30 metres. Spotted, common, striped and spinner dolphins often get trapped in these walls of death and, unable to breathe underwater, are drowned. The nets also catch whales, turtles and seabirds. As they are winched aboard the unwanted, dead animals are thrown back into the sea. These enormous nets are frequently lost, and drift around the oceans catching and drowning anything that gets in their way – Japan alone loses 16 kilometres of netting every night.

In one 13-year period an estimated 4.8 million dolphins were killed by US-registered vessels alone. Fleets from many other countries, including Japan, Taiwan, South Korea, Mexico, Venezuela, Ecuador, Spain, Costa Rica, El Salvador, Panama and the Soviet Union, also set their tuna nets around dolphins. In the United States, the Marine Mammal Protection Act now permits tuna fishing boats to kill no more than 20,500 dolphins a year. In theory, once the limit has been reached the fishing has to stop. But it is very difficult to monitor and, when the Act was passed by the US Congress, many ships were re-flagged under Latin American nations who did not have such regulations. Other countries, also without regulations, are expanding their tuna fisheries and catching increasing numbers of dolphins.

It is true that some vessels have skindivers and small boats ready to release the trapped animals, or use nets from which the porpoises and dolphins can escape more easily, and some of the dolphins themselves have altered their behaviour around fishing boats, which has also reduced mortality. But the crews of many tuna seiners do not bother to help the animals. The international tuna fishing fleet in the eastern tropical Pacific alone continues to kill 110,000 dolphins every year. At least, that is the official count; independent surveys suggest that the figure could be nearer 250,000.

Then, in 1988, another tuna fishing method was discovered by environmentalists. It involves the use of underwater explosives. Helicopters are launched from the huge fishing boats to scour the seas for dolphins. When they have found a large school, they drop bombs into the water to stun the innocent animals. The dolphins stop swimming because they are frightened and confused and, consequently, so do the tuna. Then they are all netted together. A recent report on this appalling fishing technique concluded that the bombs physically injure dolphins that happen to be swimming nearby when they explode, and cause hearing loss in dolphins over a much wider area, which means that they are unable either to communicate or to echolocate.

Many ideas have been proposed to deal with the tuna fishing problem. One is to attach electronic alarms to the nets, which would frighten the dolphins but not the fish; this may have a promising future, but is still in the early stages of development. Another is for more stringent controls; these are desperately needed, although they would probably be unenforceable in many fishing areas. But there is one particular solution which could be implemented very quickly and effectively – the introduction of laws which would require labels on tins of tuna to say how the fish were caught. Few people would buy a tin clearly marked with the message 'This tuna was caught by fishing techniques known to kill or injure dolphins'. In many conservation efforts there is no greater ally than public pressure.

Seal hunting and viruses

Seals have been hunted for thousands of years. They are very easy animals to kill because they are so clumsy on land. Their meat and fat are a source of food; their blubber can be boiled down to provide oil for heating and lighting; and their fur can be used to make warm and waterproof clothing. Eskimo, Inuit and Yupik people in many parts of the Arctic have traditionally hunted seals for subsistence, although these days they use rifles instead of harpoons and usually sell the skins for cash. Some coastal communities in other parts of the world also hunt seals in relatively small numbers.

But commercial hunting is another matter. During the last 300 years there have been some major hunts for purely commercial purposes which have had disastrous effects on seal populations.

In 1683, when the explorer William Dampier visited Juan Fernandez, a small group of islands off the coast of Chile, he noted that 'seals swarm as thick about this island, as if they had no other place to live in, for there is not a bay nor rock that one can get ashore on, but is full of them'. The first sealing vessels arrived just four years later, marking the beginning of more than two centuries of intensive exploitation. Surprisingly, the Juan Fernandez fur seals were still common when the navigator Philip Carteret arrived in 1766. He commented that 'the seals are so numerous I verily think that if many thousands of them were killed at night, they would not be missed in the morning'. But he was wrong. Dozens of sealing vessels arrived soon afterwards and began to dispatch hundreds of thousands, or even millions, of skins every year. By 1824 the sealers had practically exterminated their quarry and abandoned the islands. The Juan Fernandez fur seal was finally declared extinct in 1917. Fortunately, a few individuals had somehow survived, and the species was rediscovered in 1965. The seals were given complete protection and they are now thriving, with a relatively healthy population of 3,000–7,000.

During the same period there was seal hunting on a similar scale in Guadalupe, South Georgia, the South Orkneys and many other parts of the world. In every case, the seal populations were decimated but rescued by strenuous conservation efforts at the eleventh hour.

Restricted (but highly controversial) seal hunting still takes place in a number of countries today. Canadian harp seals and, to a lesser extent, hooded seals, have been the main focus of attention in recent years. Every spring thousands of them gather in the freezing cold waters of the North Atlantic and Arctic Oceans, where they haul out on to the ice floes to give birth. For centuries, there to greet them were hundreds of men, armed with clubs, ready to kill the pups for their valuable fur coats. In the last 250 years more than 70 million harp and hooded seals have been killed in this way. The event constantly made headline news throughout the 1970s and 1980s; pictures of the Canadian and Norwegian hunters clashing with protesters on the ice, and of people spraying live pups with coloured dyes to make them worthless, became a familiar sight across the world.

Harp seals have three main breeding grounds. They gather off the coast of Newfoundland and in the Gulf of St Lawrence, in Canada; in the Greenland Sea, on the so-called West Ice just north of the island of Jan Mayen; and also in the White Sea. Hooded seals share the first two breeding areas, but have a third in the Davis Strait, between Baffin Island and Greenland.

Most of the pelts from the baby seals taken in Canada used to go to Europe, particularly West and East Germany, Italy, Sweden, Finland and France. Britain was used as a distribution centre. The trade was based on the beautiful soft, white fur of harp seals, or whitecoats as they are known in the trade; and the silvery blue-grey fur of hooded seals, otherwise known as bluebacks.

There were international protests against the hunt from the 1950s onwards. Initially, this was entirely because of the cruelty involved; observers claimed, on numerous occasions, that the clubbing was inefficient and that many pups were being skinned alive. In particular, the fact that this was done in full view of their mothers upset a great many people. But in later years there was growing concern that the seal populations were threatened by the scale of the hunt; when the protest first began, an average of 316,000 harp seals were being killed every year. Experts were concerned that too little was known about their population to set 'safe' quotas. But many people questioned whether the seals should be harvested at all, believing that moral and emotional reasons alone should be enough to warrant their protection.

By the mid-1970s the general feeling amongst the public and many conservation groups was that the sealing should be stopped altogether. The anti-hunt campaign (which was still based mainly on cruelty rather than conservation) gathered momentum and, by the early 1980s, had managed to reduce the average number of harp seal pups being killed to just 36,000 a year, despite annual quotas of 175,000. But the Canadian government continued to promote old and hackneyed excuses to defend the hunt, a favourite being that the seals had to be culled to prevent them from competing with fisheries for declining fish stocks, and made clandestine efforts to stifle the opposition. It even introduced new regulations designed specifically to hamper protestors. The world's conservation groups, however, were unperturbed and publicly accused the government of bending the rules, juggling statistics and colouring the data.

Then in 1983 the EEC banned all sealskin imports for a trial period of two years. It was a major victory, successfully knocking the bottom out of the market and starting a chain of events which eventually led to the end of the hunt. The EEC ban was reviewed in 1985 and extended for a further four years, then reviewed again in 1989, when it was extended indefinitely. Meanwhile, the mass protest of millions of people all over the world had become too loud for the Canadian government to ignore any longer. It finally announced, on 31 December 1987 that the killing of harp seal pups was to end.

Nowadays the seals in the Gulf of St Lawrence are greeted every spring by tourists. Their annual gathering has become one of the world's wildlife spectaculars, and the money from tourism is providing local people with a welcome new source of income. For the time being, at least, the pups are relatively safe.

But the hunting of older seals is still allowed, and the Canadian Sealer's Association recently started a campaign to gain support for a larger harp seal hunt off Newfoundland. Yet again, Canadian officials are adamant that it is necessary to kill seals 'to protect the fishing industry'. They claim that the population is increasing, even though it actually fell from 10 million at the beginning of the century to some 2.5 million in the early 1980s (no one has monitored its size since). They also claim that the 'increasing numbers' are now eating too many cod and even greater numbers of capelin, which the cod eat. Indeed, fishermen all over the world blame seals for eating 'their' fish, and would like nothing more than to decimate the local seal populations. But how serious is the competition for fish?

There is no easy answer. The ocean food web is highly complex and it is difficult to determine the diet and daily food requirements of seals. But there are few convincing examples of seals affecting the abundance of fish stocks. They eat a range of different prey species and probably vary their diet according to availability. Much of their food is of no commercial importance, or is caught in regions where there are no commercial fisheries. And some of the fish they eat feed on other fish, so the presence of seals may actually result in a growth of some stocks.

Humans add stress to the ocean ecosystem by taking excessively large numbers of fish. The scale of the fishing industry has grown enormously in the last century, due to a combination of human greed, larger fishing fleets, better equipment and improved techniques; in fact in many parts of the world the fish stocks have been reduced to dangerously low levels and many people say that it is the fishermen who threaten the seals by removing their food source, not the other way around. No one denies that seals eat some commercial fish, but the proportion is usually so small that seal culling rarely produces measurable benefits for the fisheries. Also, if the seals are removed, other predators, such as dolphins and seabirds, are likely to move in to replace them. And anyhow, more fish in the marketplace does not necessarily mean increased revenues, simply because the selling price tends to drop.

Fishermen also blame seals for damaging their nets. There is no doubting that seals are intelligent animals and are quick to learn about new and productive sources of food; they steal the bait from fishing hooks, or from inside lobster pots, and rip open nets to get at the fish trapped inside. Salmon nets are most at risk, not only because they are set regularly in the same places, but also because seals, like many people, appear to have expensive tastes.

Seals damage the nets in two ways. Sometimes they follow the fish right inside and tear the mesh accidentally while struggling to get out; alternatively, they tear it deliberately, fighting to get at the fish on the inside. Either way, the damage allows trapped fish to escape and, until the damage is discovered, prevents others from being caught.

Another complaint is that the seals rarely restrict themselves to eating one or two fish, preferring to take a bite out of as many as possible instead. This adds to the losses by making the survivors less marketable. Some of the worst damage is done at coastal fish farms, where salmon and sea trout are reared in large net cages anchored in sheltered bays and inlets. The seals know that these are potential sources of plentiful food, but if they tear the nets, thousands of pounds worth of fish can escape in a matter of minutes.

The synthetic fibres used in modern nets are getting stronger so that, nowadays, the seals do less immediate damage than they once did; indeed, once trapped, they are often unable to tear themselves free, and consequently drown. But the fish damage can still be quite significant. Furthermore, it is believed that a net which has had a seal in it smells for a long time afterwards – and keeps the fish away.

But determined seals are difficult to discourage. They fight their way through extra layers of predator netting and, after a few days, even ignore killer whale calls being played underwater. Bounty schemes and organised culls have been tried, with little success, because they usually fail to remove the rogue seals causing the worst problems. The only effective measure appears to be on-the-spot protection – shooting seals caught red-handed. But even this requires constant vigilance and is almost impossible at night.

Another complication in the controversy is the fact that seals suffer from large numbers of parasites, and are accused of being involved in outbreaks of codworm, particularly in British, Norwegian and Canadian fisheries. The life cycle of the codworm begins inside the seal's stomach, where it lays its eggs. These escape in the faeces and disperse in the seawater, where they hatch. The young larvae are then eaten by tiny crustaceans, which in turn are eaten by a fish, the larvae making their way to the fleshy parts of their new host, where they wait patiently for the fish to be eaten by a seal – and the cycle begins again. But the precise relationship between the codworms, seals and fish is far from simple; in most cases there appears to be no direct correlation between seal numbers and the level of infestation in fish. However there have been exceptions in the past and, clearly, seals must be present for the fish to be affected. The codworms themselves are usually killed by freezing or cooking, which renders them harmless to people, but eating infested fish is not a pleasant thought and, if the codworms are visible, the fish are almost impossible to sell. The larvae can be removed by hand, but this adds substantially to overall costs and most fisheries, perhaps inevitably, prefer to have the seals removed instead.

The seal virus that recently killed more than 17,000 of Europe's common seals, and 300 grey seals, probably was not a direct result of human activities, but it received such widespread media coverage (partly because of the initial belief that it was caused by pollution) that it focused public attention on the problems of the marine environment. Fortunately, although the virus took a heavy toll, the common seal population was large enough to withstand its attack. But it demonstrated how easily and quickly an unforeseeable event such as this could wipe out the entire population of a much rarer animal. If a similar virus found its way to the Mediterranean, for example, where there are just 500 surviving monk seals, it could plunge the species to extinction in a matter of months, or even weeks.

Seal biologists now believe that the virus problem originated in April 1988 on the island of Anholt, in the sea between Denmark and Sweden. The first sign was the premature births of nearly 100 pups but, soon afterwards, sick adults began to appear as well. It coincided with two unrelated events which, nevertheless, fuelled speculation that pollution was responsible: a massive bloom of algae in the area, which drifted out into the North Sea; and the breeding failure of some species of seabirds in the Shetland Islands.

The disease spread rapidly and, within four months, had reached as far west as the Irish Sea. Almost all the common seal populations in Europe were affected. The speed at which it killed the animals was also staggering; one observer reported that apparently healthy and lively seals suddenly became lethargic, then started coughing, began to have breathing difficulties and nasal discharges, and were soon unable to dive underwater. Some were apparently dead within a few hours.

As the death toll mounted and hundreds of carcasses were washed ashore in several countries, the biologists struggled to find the cause. Mass deaths of this kind are very rare in seals and had never before been recorded on such a huge scale. The culprit was identified as a new virus, closely related to both human measles and canine distemper, and later named the phocine (= seal) distemper virus, or PDV. It works by attacking the immune system of the seals and making them more susceptible to other viral and bacterial infections.

Few seals died during 1989, so the survivors have probably developed some kind of resistance. But what triggered the virus in the first place? Why were grey seals not so severely affected? And, most important of all, even if pollution was not the primary cause, could some kind of toxic pollutant have contributed to the severity of the outbreak? These questions remain unanswered.

Coral reefs

Coral reefs can best be described as tropical rainforests under the sea. They are a blaze of colour and incredibly productive, supporting a fantastic variety of marine life, from fish and sea slugs to jellyfish and sea cucumbers. There are so many different animals and plants living around the reefs that new species are being discovered all the time.

Most reefs are found in the tropics and, because they need plenty of light, grow only in shallow water. They are formed by small soft-bodied creatures called polyps, which are only a couple of millimetres long and are related to jellyfish and sea anemones. A polyp is able to take the chemical calcium carbonate from seawater and use it to make a hard limestone skeleton called coral. A kind of algae, which obtains its nutrients from the polyps, then helps to build up a coral reef by cementing the different structures together – a marvellous example of a symbiotic partnership.

The reefs grow continuously in this way, the structures accumulating over thousands of years. Forming a substrate for other forms of life, they play the same role as the trees of a forest and, as they grow, are colonised by more and more animals and plants.

As well as forming the basis of rich communities of wildlife, coral reefs play several other important roles in the marine ecosystems:

- They provide nursery grounds for many species of commercially important fish.
- They act as natural barriers, helping to protect coastlines against waves and storms.
- And, like rainforests, they are natural pharmacies; many of the toxic substances produced by their inhabitants have widely applicable medical uses, from aleviating arthritis to providing potential anti-cancer drugs.

However, despite their tremendous value, coral reefs are under threat for a variety of reasons; they are fragile ecosystems and easily damaged or destroyed. In many parts of the tropics, reef fish and other animals are over-exploited, or damaging fishing methods (such as the use of explosives and poisons) are used to catch them; for example, fish collectors in the Philippines have used as much as 300 tonnes of cyanide every year to stun reef fish. Hundreds of tonnes of coral are removed from the reefs every year for the tourist curio trade; many people who buy such trinkets are probably unaware that their souvenir is the skeleton of an animal. The reefs also suffer from the effects of excessive logging and inappropriate farming techniques ashore, which lead to soil erosion; the soil is washed into rivers and is eventually flushed out into the sea, where it smothers and kills the coral. Pollution, coastal development, extraction of the reefs for building materials, and recreational activities are all taking a further toll. And a major concern for the future is rising sea levels – if the reefs are covered by too much water, they do not receive enough light, and 'drown'.

Since the early 1980s there has been a new impetus behind coral reef conservation, as demonstrated by controls on the ornamental coral and shell trades, the establishment of marine reserves, and by legislation. For example, the export of coral is now prohibited or controlled in some 30 countries, although some of the main suppliers are still flouting the regulations; one of the worst offenders is the Philippines, which exports hundreds of tonnes of coral every year, despite legislation since 1977 banning collection and exports. Worldwide trade is in the region of 2,000 tonnes every year.

Surprisingly little is known about coral reefs, particularly about their life cycles and biology. For example, it was discovered only a few years ago that half the corals on the Great Barrier Reef in Australia spawn together on a single night every year. This only goes to demonstrate that, until more information is available, it is too risky to devise strategies for the sustainable exploitation of coral on a large scale.

WHY CONSERVE WILDLIFE?

Wildlife conservation may seem almost irrelevant compared to dealing with major environmental problems such as the greenhouse effect and the destruction of the ozone layer. Many people agree that it would be a pity if animals like the giant panda or the humpback whale disappeared, although they assume that it would not be a major disaster. As for other threatened species, like the Texas blind salamander or the black bog ant, few tears would be shed if they were to become extinct.

But the truth is that wildlife conservation is very much in tune with our own survival. There are many practical reasons for caring for the ugly and obscure creatures of this world, as well as the more appealing ones. All animals and plants have a role to play in the workings of the natural environment and, whether we understand that role or not, the extinction of any species could have disastrous repercussions throughout the ecosystem. Equally important is the fact that we rely, directly or indirectly, on wildlife for our food, building materials, medicines and many other necessities of life.

But at the same time, we must not lose sight of the moral reasons for protecting animals and plants. In the modern world it is easy to forget the fact that we have a responsibility to other forms of life; all species have an inherent right to exist. We should also place more value on their presence. Animals and plants are essential for human happiness – they are interesting, attractive and inspiring. As Chief Seattle said in 1854: 'What is man without the beasts? If all the beasts were gone, man would die from a great loneliness of spirit'.

WWF's early successes included rallying international support to save the polar bear and ban commercial whaling, and working with the Indian government to protect the Bengal tiger. And species as diverse as the Arabian oryx in the Middle East and the large blue butterfly in Britain have been re-introduced.

In 1989 WWF took the lead in persuading 76 nations to ban the ivory trade – a radical move to prevent poachers from marketing the tusks from the thousands of elephants killed illegally each year in Africa. To rebuild devastated herds, WWF is providing £1.5 million of aid to eight African nations.

Illegal trade in wildlife is a constant threat to the stability of species. To combat this, WWF set up an investigation agency, TRAFFIC, to crack down on smuggling and illegal imports of species as varied as the hyacinth macaw and the chimpanzee.

6 POPULATION

WWF

For many thousands of years there were no more than five million people in the world. They lived in small hunter-gatherer bands and their numbers were limited by the same natural laws which govern all other animals. But with the advent of farming, some 10,000 years ago, the human population began to have more control over its own destiny. Human numbers rose steadily and eventually passed the 500-million mark in 1300. The industrial revolution, which began in about 1750, added a colossal spurt to the population growth; by 1830, the number of people in the world had doubled to one billion. Then it took only 100 years for it to double again to two billion. Fifty years later it had doubled again to four billion. There are now more than five billion people in the world – and the figure could double yet again by the middle of the next century.

The annual growth rate is currently 1.74 per cent, which means that, every year, the world must accommodate a new population roughly one and a half times that of Britain. The rate of increase is actually slowing, but the absolute number of people being added to the population continues to grow.

Ninety per cent of this growth over the next 50 years is expected to be in the developing world, so many of the newcomers are being born into countries already beset by poverty and food shortages. This sheer weight of numbers is placing an enormous strain on the world's natural resources, and lies at the root of many of today's environmental problems. As the old adage goes, 'Whatever your cause, it's a lost cause without population control.'

WHAT TRIGGERED THE POPULATION EXPLOSION?

There are several theories to explain why the human population is growing so rapidly.

One proposes that it is caused by the recent increases in food production. It suggests that the number of people is limited only by the availability of food and will continue to grow until the human world can no longer feed itself. But there are many flaws in this rather simplistic argument. The recent famines in Africa are cited as an example of food being the limiting factor, yet famines are caused by a combination of climatic, political and social influences, not simply a shortage of food. Perhaps most important of all, the theory implies that the fastest population growth should be in rich countries, where people have access to the most resources. In fact the reverse is true.

Another, more widely-held, belief is that the population growth has been triggered by a dramatic fall in the death rate. Medical advances, better sanitation and improvements in nutrition have reduced death rates in most parts of the world. This certainly helps to explain why Britain's population quadrupled during its rapid period of development in the 19th century. And, at first glance, it also appears to be responsible today for the mushrooming populations in many parts of the developing world. In Kenya, for example, the introduction of immunisations, antibiotics and malaria control has helped to reduce the country's death rate from 27 per 1,000 to only 12 per 1,000 in less than 40 years. Kenya's population is now growing faster (at the rate of 4 per cent every year) than in any other country in the world; currently 24 million, it is expected to double within the next 17 years. For comparison, the population doubling time in Sweden is 6,930 years.

But a fall in death rate alone cannot account for the population problems of the developing world. Britain, Sweden and other industrialised countries have even lower death rates than Kenya, yet their populations have stabilised, or are falling. Why isn't the same thing happening everywhere in the world? The answer is simple: low death rates in developing countries are combined with high birth rates. In the industrialised world, the birth rate – which is now at a level that more or less balances the number of deaths – was never as high as it is now in places like Kenya.

Many people have blamed high birth rates on religion. Certainly, it is impossible to ignore the influence of the Catholic church in Latin America, for example. But religion alone cannot be held responsible – in some Catholic societies, such as Italy, and the Canadian province of Quebec, birth rates have actually fallen.

The reason is that birth rates depend largely upon personal choice. People in the developing world choose to have more children than people in the industrialised world. But why?

Is it a form of Hobson's choice – because they do not have access to convenient, safe and effective methods of birth control? This may be true in some instances. But the fact that birth control programmes rarely work on their own (even when contraceptives are offered free of charge) suggests that there are more complex forces in operation. Women in Senegal, for example, appear to want (and have) at least eight children each, whether they have access to modern contraceptives or not.

Is it because women in developing countries have fewer rights? This is certainly a major factor. The status and self-esteem of poor women is often terribly low. The only way they can achieve any form of prestige in many countries is by marrying at a young age and having large numbers of children. They are given no freedom of choice and would find it almost impossible to challenge the authority of their husbands or of the established religion. This is one of the reasons why birth rates remain high in some Muslim countries, such as Pakistan, where women have a particularly low status. Interestingly, women on the Indonesian island of Java, which is also Muslim, have a much higher status, and the birth rate there is falling.

There are many other traditional forces influencing birth rate. For example, men often consider large families to be a sign of their virility; women, under intense social pressure, are forced to keep giving birth until they have a son. It is also traditional, in countries where infant mortality is high, to have large numbers of children on the assumption that some will not survive; now that modern health-care is more widely available, some parents tend to over-compensate.

But, most important of all, poor people choose to have large numbers of children because they are insecure. They are denied unemployment benefits, they have no personal savings and they cannot afford pensions for their old age. Their only alternative is to invest in children. In community affairs, bigger families tend to carry more weight. But children also play an active role in the household economy, helping with chores when they are young and going out to work when they are older. In the villages they take responsibility for the animals or help on the land. In the cities they earn money by selling things on street corners or by begging from tourists. And there is always the hope that 'the next one' will be clever enough to get a 'proper' office job. Children are poor people's insurance, and the more they have, the more secure they feel.

There is also the intangible benefit of parental joy. This is considered very important in many poor communities, where grief and worry are a part of everyday life. The amount of joy appears to be measured in proportion to the number of children.

With so many factors encouraging large families, it is not surprising that, in the developing world, 37 per cent of the population is under 15 years old. The worst aspect is that population growth and poverty form a vicious circle; each contributes to the other, making recovery that much more difficult.

HOW MANY PEOPLE CAN THE WORLD SUPPORT?

Biologically, the human species is a great success. It has found ways of artificially reducing the rate at which its members die and is now overrunning the earth. But the human population cannot continue to grow forever, or until there is literally no more living space for people to squeeze into; the world's life support systems will collapse long before that point is reached. The more people there are in the world, the greater the strain on the environment; more people use more natural resources and produce more waste.

But how many people can the world support, and when are we likely to reach the limit? In truth, no one has any idea. There are, however, a number of estimates, varying from a maximum population of eight billion to more than 12 billion which, either way, implies that we may not have long to go.

Perhaps we have pushed beyond the limit in some areas already. Indeed, some countries do have lower carrying capacities than others; Mauritania has a population only one-third the size of Hong Kong, living in an area 1,000 times larger, yet the people of Mauritania are stricken with poverty and malnutrition, while the people of Hong Kong are thriving. Similarly, China has half as much agricultural land per person as India, yet the Indians suffer widespread hunger while the Chinese do not.

So how do you measure how many people a country can support? If population density and hunger are not always directly related, there must be other considerations to take into account. These include how much the people consume, the natural resources available to them, their national land-use policies, the damage they do to their own environment, their wealth, and their social and political security. Realistically, there are too many unknowns and variables within these categories to make accurate assessments. In Nigeria, for example, the population is increasing at the rate of 3.4 per cent every year which means that, by the end of the next century, it will be equal roughly to the population of the entire world today. Commonsense tells us that either the birth rate will decline or the death rate will rise (or both) long before Nigeria's population reaches that five-billion mark. But what will trigger the change – and at what point – is almost impossible to say.

The fact that all countries belong to an international community must also be considered. Global environmental issues such as the greenhouse effect, the destruction of the ozone layer, rainforest clearance and species extinction are likely to play major roles in carrying capacity – and inevitably will affect some countries more adversely than others. In most cases, it is the developing world that will suffer the most.

Although industrialised countries have virtually stable populations (their average annual growth rate is only 0.4 per cent a year) they are putting a disproportionate strain on the natural world. They have populations that are wildly in excess of their own resources, but cope by using the resources of the developing countries. Rich people also devour considerably more resources than poor people; a child in the United States consumes up to 100 times more than a child in Bangladesh. And the industrialised world produces more waste and more global pollution from its power stations, factories and cars than the developing world; in 1986 there was more than one car for every two people in the United States but only one car for every 1,445 people in China.

Many experts believe that the ultimate limiting factor on population growth may be political and social instability, aggravated by environmental problems. For example, drought, poverty and war already are forcing millions of people to leave the countryside and flood into the cities, which simply cannot cope with the onslaught. Around the world, cities are swelling to unmanageable proportions; in 1900 there were just 13 cities with a population of over one million, today there are more than 230. Mexico City is the largest, with a population of 20 million that is expected to grow to 25 million by the end of the century. The worst affected are in the developing world, where in 1950 only 17 per cent of the people lived in cities; by 2020 the figure is expected to rise to 50 per cent. In Brazil, for example, the urban population already has grown from 34 per cent in 1950 to 71 per cent in 1988. And since the mid-1950s the population of Nouakchott, the capital of Mauritania, has increased 40-fold. Many of the newcomers to these cities are poor and live in slums, without essential services such as water supplies and sewage disposal. The result is high unemployment, a lower quality of life, rising crime rates, general discontent – and social and political instability.

If we leave it to nature to solve the population problem, before the end of the next century there are likely to be environmental and human catastrophes that would dwarf anything ever seen to date. But calculating how many people the world can support, in our endeavours to ensure human survival, should not be the only consideration. We must also consider our responsibility for the well-being of all the other species with which we share the planet.

CONTROLLING POPULATION GROWTH

Only 20 years ago, at the end of the 1960s, political leaders in much of the developing world considered the idea of population control as a racist or imperialist plot. But most now accept that it must be a key factor in their planning for the future.

Many governments are tackling the problem with family planning programmes which, until quite recently, were considered to be the only way of curbing population growth. Village distribution centres are established, to provide free contraceptives and advice; educational campaigns are launched to promote the notion that a family should be 'small, happy and prosperous', as the slogans in Indonesia proclaim; and, in some areas, there are even sirens which wail at the same time every day to remind women to take their pill.

Undoubtedly, there is an unmet demand for contraception in many parts of the world, and extensive family planning programmes have played a major role in declining birth rates. In Mauritius, for example, the birth rate was nearly 40 per 1,000 before family planning was actively encouraged; within eight years, the figure had dropped to below 25 per 1,000.

But family planning programmes often have little effect, or fail completely. The reason is simple: they stand or fall on their success in persuading people to use contraceptives. They do not solve the basic social and economic factors which are encouraging people to have large families. This explains why birth rates are still high in countries such as Kenya, Nepal and India, despite long and active family planning programmes.

The term 'family planning' implies that the decision about how many children to have is made within the family itself. But some countries have given up on voluntary control and have resorted to bribery. Anyone who uses contraceptives (or agrees to being sterilised) is given a financial reward or some other incentive. Considering the poverty in countries which have done this, such as India and Bangladesh, it is not surprising that people volunteer to earn some desperately needed cash.

China, which has a population of 1.1 billion (the largest in the world) has had the most stringent birth control programme in history. Its famous one-child-family policy was designed not only to end population growth in the country but to reduce the number of people to about 700 million, which is considered to be the optimum level. The policy is so stringent that Chinese couples who conceive a second child are under pressure to have an abortion because, if the child is born, they will be faced with heavy financial penalties. But the traditional preference for sons has led to a resurgence of female infanticide, and there is evidence that sterilisation has been performed compulsorily on some 'persistent offenders'. There is also growing concern that a small working population will soon be faced with supporting an enormous number of elderly people. The programme is still in operation, although some aspects have been relaxed, particularly for people in rural areas.

Indonesia has taken even more drastic action, by redistributing millions of people away from seriously overcrowded islands, such as Java, to the less populous ones. The problems being caused are enormous; for example, vast areas of rainforest have been cleared and land has been taken away from tribal minorities just to make room for the new settlers.

In the long term the world's population can be brought under control only by tackling the more complex social and economic issues which are the root cause of the problem. Successful development and successful population control depend upon one another. But the question many people are asking is will we have time to take successful action ourselves, or will nature do it for us?

'*As resources become more scarce and the quality of the environment declines still further, even more people are bound to become poor and disadvantaged.*'

HRH, The Duke of Edinburgh, KGKT,
International President of WWF.

7
WAR AND THE ENVIRONMENT

Since the end of World War II there have been 130 wars, involving more than 80 countries. They have claimed the lives of some 20 million people. The nature of these conflicts, and their impact on the natural world, varies enormously. The effects of long and destructive wars, such as in Vietnam, will linger for many years. But even minor border skirmishes can cause colossal damage to the environment, killing wildlife and destroying wild places.

Worse still, predictions about the possible use and implications of some modern-day weapons make even science-fiction stories on the subject seem understated. There are now enough nuclear weapons in the world to kill everyone many times over and, ultimately, the risk of a nuclear holocaust is considered by many to be the gravest threat life on Earth is ever likely to face.

Environmental problems themselves may lead to military conflict. The spreading of deserts, diminishing water supplies or crop failure can cause political instability, social unrest and civil war. Shared resources such as the atmosphere, Antarctica, rivers and oceans are continuing sources of international tension. But ironically, the financial burden of military defence is so high that there is often little money left for pollution control, agricultural investment or other conservation-related activities that could minimise this tension.

There are, of course, more positive points which can be made about military development. For example, a great deal of good can come as a spin-off from scientific research undertaken initially for military purposes. And in many developing countries the military is used for civilian purposes such as disaster relief and road building.

But as the diminishing health of the environment increases the potential for conflict, and as modern technology amplifies its impact, war has become a major environmental issue of growing concern.

THE HIDDEN COSTS OF WAR

War is expensive. The world spends US$ one trillion (1,000,000,000,000) a year on military 'security', equivalent to more than US$1.85 million a minute. Yet one in five of the world's population – one billion people – lives in absolute poverty.

In the 20th century alone war has claimed the lives of 99 million people. This waste of human life is staggering enough but, on top of that, a similar number administer military and defence establishments around the world, while a further half a million scientists and engineers are employed in military research and development.

Military defence also speeds up the demand for land and raw materials. At the height of World War II some 20 per cent of Britain's land surface was devoted to training and weapons testing. In certain years the military accounted for more than 40 per cent of the US consumption of thallium and titanium. Worldwide, military defence accounts for 6 per cent of global oil consumption.

Can we really afford this extravagant and destructive use of raw materials, money that might otherwise be spent more constructively, and human skills that could be put to better use, when there are so many unmet human needs in the world?

The financial burden
On a typical day in the late 1980s/early 1990s as many as 30 wars were being fought around the world and a new one begins, on average,

once every three months. Even at times of peace, all but two of the world's 200 countries – Costa Rica and Iceland – have military forces. Our growing habit of turning to armed conflict as a solution to innumerable problems means that there is an ever-present and escalating demand for weapons and ammunition. This has already turned military defence into a major industry.

The main exporters of military hardware are the United States, the Soviet Union, France, Italy, Britain and West Germany. They supply more than 90 per cent of major weapons on the world market and frequently use their stocks of armaments for economic and political bargaining power. But the watchword of the global arms trade is profit. If it is politically insensitive to supply one country with weapons, illicit deals are always possible. More than 40 countries supplied armaments to combatants in the Iran–Iraq war; 15 supplied them to both sides.

For too many countries, so-called defence spending is near the top of the national shopping list. In 1984, the year before the Band Aid appeal, Africa spent more on importing arms and ammunition than it did on importing food. This is not unusual. It is common for developing countries to spend more on military defence than welfare, health, education and the environment combined. The Ethiopian Government in 1989 spent no less than US$1.75 billion on military defence – 56 per cent of its entire annual budget.

Developed countries are little better. The United States spends more than US$1,000 each year on every citizen, to protect them from outside enemies – even though many of these people will not walk their own streets at night for fear of assault. The Soviet Union's current interest in international disarmament is partly fuelled by the crippling burden its military spending puts on the economy. In Britain, the total money raised by its top ten charities in one year is the same as the government spends on military defence in ten days.

It is not all money down the drain. Indeed, military-oriented research is responsible for a quite significant proportion of scientific and technological advances. But the fact remains that, in the absence of the military, such investment could be made directly in research, conservation or practical means of alleviating human suffering.

Just imagine what could be achieved with the world's annual defence budget. It could pay the otherwise unmanageable foreign debt burden of virtually the entire developing world. Or it could be used to combat contagious diseases, supply clean water and proper sanitation facilities worldwide, halt the spread of deserts, provide good educational facilities and eradicate malaria, with plenty left over. There are hundreds of ways in which the money could be better spent. President Eisenhower summed up the reality of defence spending when he commented, in his parting address, that 'every gun that is made, every warship launched, every rocket fired represents, in the final analysis, a theft from those who hunger and are not fed, who are cold and not clothed'.

The human burden

Worldwide, the equivalent of Europe's entire working population is involved, directly or indirectly, with military defence. Some 20 per cent of the world's 2.5 million research scientists and engineers devote their time and skills to developing new weapons and improving old ones. And many of the largest research organisations, such as Britain's Atomic Weapons Research Establishment, are concerned exclusively with military work. Most of this human endeavour is devoted to destructive aims, although some of the research and development work undertaken for military purposes has benefited people as well; for example, the need to protect troops against tropical diseases during World War II resulted in rapid progress being made in the fight against malaria.

Troop size is another aspect of the human burden. In this respect, the dramatic changes in the eastern bloc – particularly Soviet plans to cut 500,000 men from its armed forces – are cause for considerable optimism. On 26 February 1990, for example, the Soviet Union signed an agreement with Czechoslovakia to withdraw all of its 73,500 remaining troops in the country; and, astonishingly, the first tanks left the very same day.

During war, of course, even more human resources are absorbed than during times of peace, or even during military occupation. Until World War I most soldiers were professionals but, since the introduction of conscription, armies have been composed of millions of young civilians – from farms, factories and offices – creating enormous labour vacuums. At the same time, we now have such a capacity for mass destruction that more civilians die in a war than soldiers. During World War I, 5 per cent of the casualties were civilian: in wars today the average figure is 60 per cent, so the labour vacuum can last for many years afterwards.

THE ENVIRONMENTAL COST OF WAR

Since ancient times, war has been the excuse for people physically to destroy wild places and wildlife, farmland and livestock. Greek and

Roman writers have described two age-old military tactics of environmental destruction – deforestation to reduce enemy cover and crop damage to make sure opposing armies go hungry. At the time of Henry VIII, many of England's oak trees were cut down to build warships. But as technology has advanced, the scale of destruction has increased to a point where the damage is both colossal and long-lasting. Modern traditional weapons are capable of mass destruction, but the advent of chemical and nuclear weapons has introduced a new threat of total devastation.

Military conflict also creates major obstacles to conservation work. Environmental problems are the last thing politicians are concerned about at times of war. It is often impossible for scientists and conservationists to work in war-torn areas, and tension between nations makes cooperation over the conservation or sustainable development of common resources impossible.

Loss of wildlife

Britain's Ministry of Defence is one of the country's largest landowners and, as such, plays host to a wide range of animals and plants. Many of these are quite rare in other parts of the country and the MoD takes its responsibilities seriously, ensuring that they flourish on its training ranges. But at times of war, with violence and chaos the order of the day, wildlife conservation is low down the list of priorities in any country. Nature reserves and wildlife departments collapse, and the countryside swarms with large numbers of armed men.

The military coup which brought Idi Amin to power in Uganda in 1971 led to the annihilation of the country's wildlife. Rhinos and elephants were used as target practice and their horns and ivory sold to buy arms and ammunition. People were forced to poach wildlife to avoid starvation, and the game and national parks departments fell apart. The upheavals wiped out all but a handful of Uganda's rhinos and most of its elephants. In Queen Elizabeth National Park (until recently known as Ruwenzori) there were 2,731 elephants in 1973; by 1980, a year after Amin's regime collapsed, there were just 150 left alive.

Conservation work in war-torn areas is often impossible, even after the fighting has subsided. The kouprey is a pertinent example. An extremely rare ox which lives in the forests of Cambodia, Laos, Thailand and Vietnam, it somehow survived the Vietnam War (though not unscathed) and will continue to suffer in Cambodia as the conflict there continues. The population is already down to between 100 and 300 animals but it is virtually impossible to take action to save them. They live in areas riddled with unexploded bombs and mines. Indeed, conditions are so bad that kouprey surveys along the Thai/Laos border recently had to be abandoned when one of the rangers stepped on a landmine.

Unexploded mines, bombs and bullets are a familiar post-war legacy in many countries. Left behind after the fighting, they lack built-in devices of self-destruction and can lie in the ground for decades. Many are fitted with booby-traps, designed to detonate as soon as they are tampered with. These unexploded remnants are currently a problem in many countries of the Middle East, Libya, Vietnam, Laos, the Falkland Islands and elsewhere. In Libya, they have killed more than 4,000 people since World War II, and unknown numbers of animals. In Poland, where 14.5 million mines have been cleared since the end of World War II, an incredible 300,000–400,000 are still being removed every year.

Military uses of animals and microorganisms

For thousands of years, animals have been used at times of conflict. The Roman writer Lucretius tells of lions and savage boars being launched against enemy forces. Hannibal, most famous for his use of elephants during war, also ordered earthenware pots containing poisonous vipers to be flung on to the decks of King Prusius' ships. And the world's largest empire, conquered by Genghis Khan's nomadic warriors, was overrun by armies on horseback. In modern times, animals are still being used for military tasks. The US Navy uses dolphins for military purposes, because they are intelligent, easy to train and respond well to people. They are used to recover torpedoes, by diving down and attaching cables to them; to guard Trident submarine bases; for laying mines; and even for attacking enemy frogmen.

But perhaps the most frightening developments have been in biological warfare – the use of disease-carrying microorganisms.

Biological weapons have been used for more than 700 years. When Genghis Khan was laying siege to various towns during his empire-building, he ordered his warriors to catapult diseased bodies over the town walls. And plague was introduced as a biological weapon as long ago as the 14th century. More recently, in World War I, the Germans infected allied cavalry horses with bacteria causing a highly contagious disease called glanders, and the Japanese used plague bacteria against cities in north China during the 1930s.

Biological weapons are difficult to handle and slow to take effect, but are relatively cheap to produce and are regarded by some countries as affordable weapons of mass destruction. Nowadays, any country with a modest budget can construct its own lethal bacteria and viruses against which people would have little or no resistance. These can be added to water or food supplies, dropped by bombers or delivered in the warheads of missiles. Once released, the consequences are unpredictable but potentially very serious and difficult to control.

Biological warfare is officially banned by the 1975 Biological Weapon Convention and the major powers have destroyed stocks of biological weapons. In the United States, their facilities were converted for civilian medical research. But research to develop new strains does continue; at the very least, there is still the risk of an accidental escape of lethal agents from a biological warfare laboratory.

Pockmarking the landscape
Warfare often results in considerable physical damage to the environment. The resilience of nature has smoothed over some of this damage, such as many of the earthworks of World War I battlefields, but modern wars are so destructive that the new scars are likely to be more permanent.

The most destruction has been wreaked by the use of explosive devices. In the early 1950s nearly three million tonnes of munitions were unleashed on Korea alone, and during World War II eight million tonnes were dropped on Europe.

But worse was still to come. A deluge of bombs and artillery shells, weighing a total of 15 million tonnes and equivalent to 450 times the energy of the Hiroshima atom bomb, were dropped during the Vietnam War. They resulted in some 25 million craters, some up to 30 yards wide. Many of them filled with stagnant rainwater and formed ideal new breeding grounds for malarial mosquitos. They still pockmark the landscape over thousands of square miles. Gradually, millions of farmers are filling them in, covering them with crops or even converting them into fish ponds. But the land will bear the scars of war for a long time to come.

The Iran–Iraq War was particularly destructive, with oil at the heart of the conflict and bombing raids against oil installations and tankers a major source of friction. Oil pollution in the Gulf has reached a critical level, causing serious damage to many coastal areas and threatening marine life.

The simple logistics of moving large numbers of men and heavy machinery leave their mark too. Fighting in the deserts and semi-arid parts of North Africa during World War II caused severe damage to the environment. Tanks and heavy trucks, carrying troops or weapons, destroyed the vegetation and exposed the fragile soils, which were quickly blown away.

Armies often make deliberate changes to the environment in pursuit of their military goals. Rivers were diverted during the Iran–Iraq war, flooding large areas of Iraq's eastern border, to make advances more difficult. China's Great Wall and Hadrian's Wall in northern Britain, built to keep marauding barbarians at bay, are clearly in evidence many hundreds of years after they were erected. Similar constructions are still used today; Morocco has built an earth wall as a defence against Polisario guerillas in Western Sahara, and Israel has dug ditch-and-bank defences on its northern flank.

Environmental destruction is also a military technique aimed at denying food to the enemy and its sympathetic civilians. It is not a new idea. In Biblical times Samson tied burning torches to the tails of 300 foxes and sent them into the grainfields, vineyards and olive groves of the Philistines. Enemy water sources have been poisoned for centuries and, during the 1980s, Soviet troops intentionally destroyed vegetation and crops in their fight against resistance forces in Afghanistan.

All troops need to be fed. Grenades are used as a foolproof means of killing and catching fish and other animals, while the land is stripped of fruit and crops. Habitat destruction is also caused by the building of airstrips, military access roads or even by clearing enemy hideouts. This has been a major problem in Central America, particularly in Guatemala, where Indians in the Chichicastenango region have complained that over half of their forests have been destroyed. Forests are especially vulnerable, because they hide the enemy; they are destroyed wherever guerilla activity is likely – and on no greater scale than with chemical weapons in South Vietnam.

Chemical weapons

From the mid-1960s to the early 1970s, the United States sent planes loaded with herbicides to south-east Asia. They sprayed, from the air, more than 72 million litres of these deadly chemicals on to the forests and farmland of South Vietnam. Called Operation Ranch Hand, these repeated attacks had devastating ecological, economic and social consequences in the region. Scientists who studied the tragic aftermath coined a new term – ecocide. It means killing the environment. Chemical weapons were first used in World War I, when chlorine, phosgene and mustard gas were released by both sides to kill 100,000 people and injure another million. But Operation Ranch Hand was the first massive employment of herbicides in the history of war.

Three major chemical warfare agents were used – Agents Orange, White and Blue. Agent Orange and Agent White accounted for 61 per cent and 28 per cent, respectively, of the total volume dropped. They were aimed mainly at forests. Agent Blue accounted for 11 per cent and was used mainly for crop destruction missions. The chemicals were sprayed over thousands of square kilometres – some 10 per cent of South Vietnam – but actually affected an area several times that size, because the deadly sprays were carried on the wind. A third of the targets were attacked more than once. Many were sprayed repeatedly.

The theory behind Operation Ranch Hand was that guerilla warfare would be impossible without cover, so it was decided to turn Vietnam's tropical forests into desert. It was designed to make jungle warfare much easier to combat because, with no vegetation to hide behind, the Viet Cong could be seen. At the same time, farmland spraying destroyed food crops making life impossible for the peasants and striking at the root of national resistance.

Agents Orange, White and Blue are defoliants, designed to make the leaves fall off trees. And their immediate effects were obvious. Vast areas of tropical forest and cropland were destroyed. The ecosystem most damaged was the mangrove forest of the Mekong Delta; over 40 per cent of this productive woodland and fisheries area was completely obliterated. In many areas, within a few days of spraying, villagers were reporting large number of dead animals. Agent Orange contains traces of Dioxin, an extremely toxic poison that is lethal in minute doses. The total amount used was probably only between 170 and 500 kilograms, but the only animals which survived in large numbers were rodents – and they caused sudden disease epidemics. In sublethal quantities, Dioxin can result in birth defects, genetic damage and cancers. Vietnam veterans exposed to it for long periods during the war were at risk of passing on abnormalities to their children many years after they left the contaminated areas. The consequences are even worse for the Vietnamese, who had to remain behind. Dioxin is very resistant and exists in nature for a long time. It still persists more than 25 years after its last application – in the soil and even in human breastmilk. No one knows when it will decompose.

Ironically, in some areas peasant farmers took advantage of the fall of leaves and were quick to move into the herbicide-sprayed areas. The leaf fall added nutrients to the soil and allowed sunlight to penetrate the canopy. For a while, the land was actually more productive than if the trees had been cut down by the farmers themselves. But the long-term damage caused by the spraying missions, although still being assessed, is considerable. Many of the forests will never recover. The composition of the soil has changed, essential microorganisms have disappeared, noxious plants took over before the native species could regain a foothold, or the unprotected soils have simply blown away. Some of the toxic chemicals were washed to other areas, even other countries, far from the sites of the original spraying.

The A Luoi valley is a sadly apt example of the devastation wreaked by Operation Ranch Hand. It was once a luxuriant tropical forest, teeming with wildlife. There were as many as 170 different birds and more than 30 mammals, including elephants, Javan rhinos, gaur, tigers, clouded leopards and a variety of primates. But the forest saw fierce fighting during the war and defoliants, bombs and shells were poured on to it for many years. Nearly 150 species of birds, all the large mammals and tens of thousands of cattle were lost. All that remains today is a desert of grass – dubbed by the Vietnamese as American grass – and a charred and stunted forest of bare tree stumps.

Only after years of experimentation have Vietnamese scientists pioneered the first successful replanting of a tropical forest and have finally begun to rehabilitate the country's war-ravaged environment. Their work offers hope for the rest of the tropical world. But it is unlikely that the original wealth of wildlife will ever return and it will take decades, or even centuries, for the forests themselves to regenerate properly. Some never will.

The United States and the Soviet Union reportedly each have enough chemical weapons to kill everyone in the world 300 times over. Many developing countries also have them. It was reported recently that Libya has been producing large quantities of mustard gas which, when released as a fine spray, causes serious skin blisters, blindness and (if inhaled) fatal damage to the lungs. The most hideous is the binary nerve gas which, even at extremely low concentrations, is lethal instantaneously. And even more toxic agents are being developed; these are earning themselves the reputation as the poor people's nuclear weapons – and, ironically, it is likely that a significant chemical attack would be answered with the real thing.

NUCLEAR WAR

Governments have repeatedly lied to the public about nuclear weapons. They claim that they are a necessary evil, that there is no alternative to the delicate balance of terror that they call mutual deterrence. They have lulled people into such a false sense of security that many believe the chances of a nuclear war ever happening are remote. But after 50 years of false promises, do we really have security and peace?

Many people believe that the likelihood of global nuclear war is actually increasing. Mutual deterrence is based on mutual assured destruction – a fear of retaliation – but modern weapons are so accurate that the main targets are no longer sprawling cities but relatively small weapons silos. So it is possible that military thinking is based increasingly on the belief that there is a good chance of knocking out most of the enemy's nuclear forces before they can be fired.

However, there is also a considerable body of opinion that believes that nuclear deterrence is working. Even if the concept of a fear of retaliation loses some of its relevance with technological development in weaponry, it is probably too simplistic to say that it has failed simply because it has not ended all conflict.

There are now 11 countries with nuclear weapons, or the ability to make them – the United States, the Soviet Union, Britain, France, China, Pakistan, South Africa, Israel, India, Brazil and Argentina. Libya, Iran, Iraq, and North Korea are not far behind. The two superpowers control most of these weapons and neither the United States nor the Soviet Union is likely to launch a nuclear attack on the other out of the blue. But there are several ways in which a full-scale nuclear war might begin.

A regional conflict in an area of mutual interest, such as the oil-rich Middle East or the Gulf, could escalate beyond control. Experience has demonstrated on many occasions that it is unrealistic to assume that leaders will always behave rationally. Indeed, in the history of war, all weapons (even those which once acted as effective deterrents) have eventually been wielded in anger.

Despite recent moves towards disarmament, nuclear weapons technology is spreading to countries which are politically unstable and have less stringent safeguards. Therefore the number of minor events that could lead ultimately to nuclear war is likely to increase. Worse still, since the design of nuclear weapons is no longer a secret, there is a genuine risk of terrorists manufacturing their own.

The fact that neither computers nor people are infallible is also a threat. Misunderstandings and accidents do happen, sometimes with disastrous results – like the Soviet destruction of the South Korean airliner in 1983. But with nuclear warheads in play, the stakes are considerably higher. And the military certainly does have nuclear accidents, although they are generally kept secret or the information about them is restricted. In 1961, during a routine training mission in North Carolina, a B-52 bomber automatically jettisoned two multi-megatonne nuclear weapons after one of its wings had begun to break apart. The parachute attached to one of them opened and it was later found hanging from a tree. The other hit the ground and fell apart; five of its six safety switches had been set off by the fall – only one prevented it from detonating. In 1980 a computer chip costing less than 25 pence malfunctioned and, indicating that a Soviet missile attack had begun, caused a nuclear alert in the United States. Fortunately the error was identified before retaliatory measures had been taken. But this was partly because an attack was not expected. In times of international tension the analysis of a similar warning could be very different.

Missiles explode, tests go wrong, bombers crash, submarines collide. Greenpeace has estimated that accidents, crashes and deliberate dumping have already put 60 nuclear weapons and six nuclear submarines, with 10 reactors, on the ocean bed, their radioactive contents slowly being released into the sea.

There is also a risk of individuals who handle strategic weapons, for example on nuclear submarines, behaving irrationally or irresponsibly. In October 1958 a Master Sergeant at RAF Sculthorpe, a USAF base in Britain, had a nervous breakdown. He locked himself in a nuclear weapons store and threatened to commit suicide by detonating one of the weapons. There are now many stringent measures to reduce the risk of this happening again, or of any other 'unauthorised' use. But the extent to which they guarantee future safety is a subject for intense debate. The main concern is that there is little room for manoeuvre since a single accident could cause mass destruction and even escalate to full-scale nuclear war.

Meanwhile, the testing of nuclear weapons poses its own threat. The first ever test took place in New Mexico, United States, in July 1945. It was reported at the time that the air over an area as large as Australia was contaminated with radioactivity. During the next 40 years there were 1,522 nuclear test explosions. Nearly a third of them were above ground and have caused the dispersion of radioactive material around the globe. The Pacific Ocean has long been a favourite testing ground and the effects on people and wildlife there have been appalling. Arms control treaties prohibit nuclear weapons testing in the atmosphere, outer space, Antarctica and under the sea, but underground testing continues.

Two nuclear bombs have been used in warfare. They were small by today's standards but demonstrated the terrible destruction possible and were a measure of the sinister potential of the nuclear age. A primitive uranium bomb, nicknamed 'Little Boy', was used on Hiroshima on 6 August 1945. It had an explosive power equivalent to 13,000 tonnes of TNT. Hiroshima at the time had a population of 255,000; 45,000 people died on the first day and a further 19,000 died in the following four months; 72,000 people were injured and 90 per cent of the city was demolished. Three days later a plutonium bomb, nicknamed 'Fat Man', was used on Nagasaki, which had a population of 174,000. Its explosive power was equivalent to 20,000 tonnes of TNT: 22,000 people died on the first day and a further 17,000 in the following four months; 25,000 people were injured. At the time, the world under-estimated the power of the two bombs; almost everyone believed that they were just awe-inspiringly destructive versions of ordinary weapons. But a silent and invisible cause of death persisted long after the conventional blasts and fires. It was radiation or, as one British journalist at the time called it, the 'atomic plague'. Many people died horrible deaths and, in some cases, it took years for the symptons of radiation-linked illnesses to become apparent.

Today it is possible to deliver a nuclear warhead many times as powerful in a 20 cm artillery shell. A single nuclear bomb can have an explosive power greater than that of all the explosives ever used in wars since the invention of gunpowder. In total, the power of the world's nuclear arsenals is equivalent to well over a million Hiroshimas – comparable to 3 tonnes of TNT for every person on Earth.

With weaponry on this scale, the likely consequences of nuclear war make other threats to the environment pale into insignificance. It threatens the survival of all life on Earth.

Nuclear terminology explained

An atom is one of the tiniest parts of an element. It contains an enormous amount of energy, which can be released in two different ways. One is by splitting the atom into two or more parts; this is called nuclear fission. The other is by combining one atom with another; this is called nuclear fusion.

The release of energy can be controlled and harnessed as a source of power, or uncontrolled and released in a few seconds as a massive explosion. Nuclear power stations use the energy from fission to produce heat and, ultimately, steam which is used to drive a turbine in exactly the same way as in a coal-fired power station. Nuclear weapons use either fission or fusion (or a combination of the two) to yield huge quantities of heat, light, blast and radiation in enormous explosions. Atom bombs, like the one dropped on Hiroshima, use fission; hydrogen, or thermonuclear, bombs use both fusion and fission. The power of these is measured in kilotonnes (thousands of tonnes) or megatonnes (millions of tonnes) of conventional TNT.

The initial development of both nuclear fission and nuclear fusion was for military use. But atoms for war and atoms for peace can never be considered separately. In some respects they are the opposite of one another, but the point is that any country which generates its own nuclear power could manufacture its own nuclear weapons.

The main element used in nuclear power stations is uranium, which is mined in the same way as other materials, albeit with additional safety precautions. There are significant uranium deposits in several countries notably the United States, the Soviet Union, South Africa, Australia, Canada and Zaire. Unfortunately, uranium is also a crucial element in nuclear weapons – it was the main ingredient of the atom bomb dropped on Hiroshima. A second element, plutonium, is formed as a byproduct in the power stations. This was used in the bomb dropped on Nagasaki. One of the most toxic substances known, plutonium does exist in natural ores, but in such tiny quantities that it has to be obtained artificially to meet the world demand.

Both plutonium and uranium are radioactive – they give off energy in the form of tiny subatomic particles. Radioactivity is a naturally-occurring phenomenon, caused by certain atoms changing their structure; it cannot be seen or heard but we are exposed to it all the time from rocks, the soil, buildings and even one another. Used correctly, it has many medical applications. But over-exposure to radiation can be harmful. High doses can lead to what is known as radiation sickness; in the short term this causes nausea and vomiting, diarrhoea and internal bleeding, but the worst effects can take decades to reveal themselves and, in the long term, include loss of hair, genetic abnormalities and birth defects, cancer and ultimately death.

Exploding nuclear weapons emit highly dangerous levels of radiation. The radioactive particles can be deposited from the atmosphere over a period of several years in what is called the radioactive fallout. Neutron (or enhanced radiation) bombs are designed specifically to maximise the level of radiation; they are lethal to all forms of life but have a reduced blast which leaves buildings and other structures relatively undamaged.

The carefully refined nuclear materials and fuses used in such bombs are assembled in what is called a nuclear warhead. A warhead fully integrated with its delivery system – a missile, a bomb, a shell or a landmine – is the nuclear weapon. The most crucial advances in nuclear weapons nowadays are concerned with the delivery systems. They are getting faster and more accurate all the time; missiles from either superpower could reach their adversaries within 15 minutes, hitting to within a few hundred metres of their targets.

Nuclear testing

For nearly 40 years after the Hiroshima and Nagasaki bombs had been dropped on Japan, nuclear weapons were routinely tested above ground by the United States, the Soviet Union, Britain, France and other countries. These tests released more than 200 million tonnes of radioactive fission products into the atmosphere. Many of these tests – some 500 in total – were in remote deserts or on islands in the Pacific Ocean. But the radioactive fallout was carried high into the air and drifted thousands of kilometres to other parts of the world. Wind patterns have caused much of it to rain down in the northern tundra of Scandinavia, Alaska, Canada and the Soviet Union. But the radioactive particles have contaminated every single part of the world, and the body of every human being now contains substances from the fallout – radioactivity that does not exist in nature. Some of the radioactivity has not yet even reached the Earth. When it does, there could be enough radiation to cause fatal cancers and genetic defects in thousand of people. No one knows what other, hidden harm it will do.

There was one particular test, in 1954, which probably alerted the world to the dangers of atmospheric testing more than any other. An American experiment codenamed 'Bravo', it was the explosion of the first full-scale hydrogen bomb. The site chosen for the test was Bikini, a small group of islands in the Pacific Ocean. The bomb was 1,000 times more powerful than the one that destroyed Hiroshima and produced a huge crater 75 metres deep and 1,800 metres across.

People living on the island of Rongelap, only 160 kilometres away, were not warned about the test. Some say that this was deliberate – that the islanders were being used as nuclear guinea-pigs. Within a few hours they were literally being snowed upon by radioactive debris. It settled on the ground more than an inch deep. The following day everyone had burns on their skin (which was gradually changing colour) and they showed symptoms of acute radiation sickness. Their fingernails dropped off and their hair fell out. Even today, the young children grow more slowly than normal. Their parents are experiencing an abnormally high level of thyroid cancer and leukaemia and they have one of the highest rates of diabetes in the world. Miscarriages are commonplace and babies are born dead or grotesquely deformed.

On 10 October 1963 atmospheric testing of nuclear weapons was officially banned under the Partial Test Ban Treaty, although several countries (notably France and China) continued to explode bombs above ground for years afterwards. Nuclear weapons testing today is restricted to underground experiments. Dozens of these tests are conducted every year. The explosions often send shock waves for miles and blast huge craters in the ground. On many occasions, they have even triggered earthquakes. There is nothing to ban underground testing (except in Antarctica) yet the only difference with atmospheric testing is that, instead of being released into the air, the radioactivity is mostly – but by no means entirely – trapped in the earth.

Nuclear winter

Great uncertainties remain about the aftermath of a nuclear war. But experts in both the United States and the Soviet Union have, independently, reached similar conclusions – that in a significant exchange there would be a serious possibility of human extinction.

In a highly charged atmosphere of international conflict, a nuclear war is likely to be quite substantial. Most studies have been based on exchanges of 5,000–6,500 megatonnes, or slightly less than half the world's nuclear arsenal. We can only make an informed guess at the sequence of events after such a nuclear exchange, but no one can fail to be convinced of the horror of its possible effects.

Here is one commonly quoted scenario. The war itself would be over in a few hours. Even in the northern hemisphere, where the majority of nuclear targets are located, a significant number of people, animals and plants would probably survive the immediate effects of the explosions. But the principal threat to life would come in the aftermath.

Each explosion would be accompanied by a silent wave of intense heat and a flash of light hundreds of times brighter than the sun. A shock-wave of extreme pressure and hurricane-force winds would follow. Electromagnetic pulses from the bombs would put electric power grids out of action and communications systems would collapse.

But most important of all, there would be uncontrollable fire-storms on a gigantic scale. These huge fires would eject nearly 200 million tonnes of soot and ash into the atmosphere within two days, having a devasting effect on the global climate. A similar situation may have caused the extinction of the dinosaurs 60 million years ago; there is a popular theory that they died out after an enormous meteor struck the Earth with such force that massive amounts of dust were thrown into the atmosphere, cutting off the light and warmth from the sun. Even today, we witness volcanic eruptions throwing huge clouds of soot and ash into the air that have significant meteorological effects.

Within two weeks of a nuclear exchange, the growing blanket of soot and ash would block out as much as 99 per cent of the sunlight over the northern hemisphere, causing extreme darkness and cold. If it were to cross the equator, which is considered likely, the entire world would be in the grip of what is called a nuclear winter. The planet would be virtually uninhabitable for six months or more.

A fall of only a few degrees centigrade in average world temperatures would threaten all the world's tropical rain forests and would result in snow falling in Britain in the middle of summer. But in a nuclear winter the temperature would drop to a minimum of minus 15 °C. It might drop to as much as minus 40 °C. Few animals or plants could survive for long in temperatures this low.

If the northern hemisphere was not utterly destroyed, starvation would be an immediate problem. Crops would die because of the freezing temperatures and lack of sunlight, and radioactive fallout from the blast would cause rainwater and stored food to become deadly poisonous. Acute radiation sickness would be rife; sub-lethal doses would possibly lead to a suppression of the immune system similar to that caused by AIDS, making people more susceptible to infectious disease. The synergistic effect of malnutrition, disease, physical trauma and stress would probably make most people so confused and shocked that they would either go insane or enter into a state of apathy and inaction.

The southern hemisphere would begin to collapse as well, even if it totally avoided nuclear attack. Long before being engulfed by the approaching nuclear winter, it would suffer the consequences of a complete breakdown in international trade in food, fertilisers and fuel.

When the dust and ash finally begins to clear, there would be new problems to contend with. Vast quantities of nitrogen oxides, produced by the fires, will have eaten up 30–70 per cent of the ozone in the upper atmosphere. This would increase the amount of harmful ultraviolet light reaching the Earth, causing blindness or giving everyone a potentially lethal dose of sunburn.

This popular image of a nuclear holocaust, painted by experts in both East and West, suggests that there would be nowhere to hide. Yet governments tell us about recovery after a nuclear war. Is it really feasible? Admittedly, no one can be certain about the effects of a nuclear winter – and some experts have discredited the idea altogether – but the accumulated evidence is too much to ignore.

KEEPING THE PEACE

There are many sources of conflict in the world. Religion, human rights violations, struggles for national independence and the ideological differences between East and West have all caused unrest many times in the past and will continue to do so in the future. But environmental problems are accentuating and precipitating political discontent and international grievances in many parts of the world.

The uneven distribution of resources is a major source of conflict. Apartheid in South Africa increases environmental degradation by allocating, through the homelands system, 14 per cent of the nation's land to 72 per cent of its population. This adds to existing political unrest. In the Middle East hydroelectric plans have brought neighbouring states to the brink of war. And in Europe, in the early 1970s, dispute over the rich fishing grounds of the North Atlantic led to the so-called 'cod war' between Britain and Iceland.

Ecological disasters (and war) cause mass movements of refugees which swarm across national borders, heightening interstate tensions, or swelling already overcrowded shanty towns to bursting point; Sudan, for example, is host to more than two million refugees – 70,000 who have fled from Chad, 5,000 from Uganda, 1.5 million of its own people displaced by civil war, and 630,0000 Eritreans. There is strong evidence to suggest that movements of this kind have triggered a great deal of unrest in a number of Sahelian countries.

Competition for shared resources also has potential for conflict. If global warming causes a significant rise in the world's sea levels, major shifts would occur in national boundaries between coastal nations and in the strategic importance of international waterways.

In many of these instances, security could be improved more effectively through careful environmental management than through expenditure on military defence. The precise links between the environment and political and social unrest are complex and poorly understood but, as many national leaders are beginning to realise, the two are inseparable. Real security depends upon environmental security.

This is a monumental challenge. It requires a new spirit of international cooperation. But unless major environmental problems can be solved, all conventional efforts to attain world peace will undoubtedly fail.

When wars end, resources are needed to restore the shattered environment. WWF has actively supported Vietnam's national conservation strategy, and awarded its coveted Gold Medal to Professor Vo Quy, an eminent Vietnamese conservationist, for his work in restoring the country's resources.

Occasionally, wars can allow wildlife to flourish in an area man cannot enter. Following the end of the Cold War and the disappearance of the Iron Curtain, WWF has opened an office in East Germany. One of its priorities is to assess and conserve the wildlife which has flourished for over 40 years in the prohibited zone between the two Germanys.

BIBLIOGRAPHY

I have consulted innumerable articles, scientific papers and books while researching for *The WWF Environment Handbook*. It would serve little purpose to list them all here, but several sources have been particularly useful: *The Economist, New Scientist, Ambio, Scientific American, Geographical Magazine, Oryx, BBC Wildlife, Green Magazine, IUCN Bulletin, The Guardian* and *The Sunday Times*. I have also drawn from a number of WWF publications, including *WWF News, WWF Features* and various internal and external reports. For anyone interested in finding out more about some of the subjects mentioned, the following books are excellent:

Barnaby, Dr Frank, *The Gaia Peace Atlas*, Pan 1988.
Caufield, Catherine, *In the Rainforest*, Heinemann 1985.
Goldsmith, Edward, and Nicholas Hildyard, *The Earth Report 2*, Mitchell Beazley 1990.
Lappe, Frances Moor, and Rachel Schurman, *Taking Population Seriously*, Earthscan 1989.

SELECTED BIBLIOGRAPHY

May, John, *The Greenpeace Book of the Nuclear Age*, Victor
Gollancz 1989.
McKibben, Bill, *The End of Nature*, Viking 1990.
Reader's Digest, *Antarctica*, 1985.

ABOUT THE WORLD WIDE FUND FOR NATURE

Founded in 1961 by a group of dedicated conservationists – including Sir Peter Scott – WWF is now the largest independent conservation group in the world. It has over 3 million supporters around the globe and is actively working on every continent to curb environmental destruction.

WWF has changed in the three decades of its existence from an organisation concerned primarily about species, to one striving to stop the destruction of the world's natural resources. Worldwide, WWF itself spends more than £40 million a year on conservation, as well as working to persuade governments, aid agencies and the public to give environmental concerns higher priority.

INTERNATIONAL WWF ADDRESSES

WWF — Australia
Level 17, St Martin's
Tower
31 Market Street
GPO Box 528
Sydney NSW 2001

**WWF — Australia
(Victoria)**
2nd Floor
Ross House
247–251 Flinders Lane
Melbourne VIC 3000

WWF — Austria
Ottakringerstrasse
114–116/9
Postfach 1
1162 Vienna

WWF — Belgium
608 Chauseée de Waterloo
1060 Brussels

WWF — Canada
60 St Clair Avenue East
Suite 201
Toronto
Ontario M4T 1N5

WWF — Denmark
Ryesgade 3
2200 Copenhagen N

WWF — Finland
Uudenmaankatu 40
00120 Helsinki 12

WWF — France
151 Boulevard de la Reine
78000 Versailles

WWF — Germany
Hedderichstrasse 110
PO Box 70 11 27
6000 Frankfurt a/M 70

WWF — Hong Kong
The French Mission
1 Battery Path
Central
Hong Kong

WWF — India
c/o Godrej & Boyce Ltd
Lalbaug
Parel
Bombay 400 012

**WWF — India/
New Delhi Office**
Attn: Ms Abha Singh
Export Products Division
WWF – India
B-1 Local Shopping Centre
J-Block
Saket
New Delhi–110 017

WWF — Italy
Via Salaria 290/221
00199 Roma

**WWF — Italy/
Milan Office**
Via Donatello 5/B
20131 Milan

WWF — Japan
Nihonseimei Akabanebashi
Building 7F, 3-1-14 Shiba
Minato-ku
Tokyo 105

WWF — Malaysia
PO Box 10769
50724 Kuala Lumpur

WWF — Netherlands
Postbus 7
3700 AA Zeist

WWF — New Zealand
35 Taranaki Street, 2/F
PO Box 6237
Wellington

WWF — Norway
Hegdehaugsveien 22
0167 Oslo 1

WWF — Pakistan
PO Box 1312
Lahore

**WWF — Pakistan/
Karachi Office**
1 Bath Island Road
Karachi 0402

WWF — South Africa
PO Box 456
Stellenbosch 7600

WWF — Spain
6 Santa Engracia
Madrid 10

WWF — Sweden
Ulriksdals Slott
171 71 Solna

WWF — Switzerland
Förrlibuckstrasse 66
Postfach, 8037 Zürich

**WWF — Switzerland/
Geneva Office**
14 Chemin de Poussy
1214 Vernier-Genève

**WWF — United
Kingdom**
Panda House
Weyside Park
Godalming
Surrey GU7 1XR
Tel: (0483) 426444

WWF — United States
1250 24th Street N.W.
Washington DC 20037

WWF — International
Avenue du Mont-Blanc
1196 Gland
Switzerland

INDEX

WWF

JOIN OUR FIGHT FOR NATURE TODAY

WWF members' annual subscriptions provide the vital support which is necessary for us to campaign, inform the public and lobby governments on critical environmental issues. Send us £15 for your first year of membership, and we will make sure you are kept up to date with our work by sending you WWF News every quarter. Just send the coupon below together with your payment to: WWF United Kingdom, FREEPOST, Godalming, Surrey GU7 1BR. No stamp is needed – but if you use one even more of our precious funds will go to save our natural world.

61V

YES, I would like to join WWF. Please send my membership pack. I enclose a cheque/postal order (made payable to WWF United Kingdom) for £15

OR Please debit this amount from my Access/Visa Card (delete as appropriate).

Card Number

Mr/Mrs/Miss/Ms _____
(BLOCK LETTERS)

Address _____

_____

Postcode _____ Tel. No. _____
(include STD code)

Signature _____

☐ Tick if under 18 years